Mexicans
IN WISCONSIN

Sergio M. González

WISCONSIN HISTORICAL SOCIETY PRESS

Published by the Wisconsin Historical Society Press
Publishers since 1855
The Wisconsin Historical Society helps people connect to the past
by collecting, preserving, and sharing stories. Founded in 1846,
the Society is one of the nation's finest historical institutions.
Join the Wisconsin Historical Society: wisconsinhistory.org/membership

Front cover: A family of migrant cherry workers in Door County.
WHI IMAGE ID 18938
Back cover: Jesus Salas and Lupe Martinez are depicted in a section of a mural at First
and Mitchell Streets in Milwaukee. The ten-by-eighty-five-foot mural completed in
2017 highlights the stories of migrant workers and Mexican American immigrants.
It was created by lead artist Raoul Deal of the University of Wisconsin–Milwaukee
Peck School of Arts, four undergraduate research assistants, and ten high school
interns from Artworks for Milwaukee. Courtesy of Raoul Deal

Printed in Canada
Designed by Jane Tenenbaum

21 20 19 18 17   1 2 3 4 5

Library of Congress Cataloging-in-Publication Data
González, Sergio M., 1987—author.
Mexicans in Wisconsin / Sergio M. González.
1st edition. | Madison : Wisconsin Historical Society Press, [1987] |
LCCN 2017016088 (print) | LCCN 2017016660 (ebook) | ISBN
9780870208355 (Ebook) | ISBN 9780870208348 (pbk. : alk. paper)
Subjects: LCSH: Mexicans—Wisconsin—History—20th century. |
Mexicans—Wisconsin—Social conditions. | Mexicans—Wisconsin—Politics
and government. | Migrant labor—Wisconsin.
LCC F395.M5 (ebook) | LCC F395.M5 G64 2017 (print) | DDC
305.868/720775—dc23
LC record available at https://lccn.loc.gov/2017016088

To my parents, Bertha and Sergio Armando,
who traveled different paths from Mexico to make
Wisconsin our home. Their stories inspired this book.

Milwaukee County Historical Society

Accomplished musician and composer Raphael Baez was the first known Mexican to settle in Wisconsin. He came to the United States with a touring company in 1884 and lived in Milwaukee from 1886 to his death in 1931.

WISCONSIN'S FIRST MEXICANO

A classically trained musician from a southern state in Mexico was perhaps the first Mexican ever to call Wisconsin home. Born in Puebla, Mexico, on May 15, 1863, Raphael Baez was the son of Jose de la Luz Baez, whose family had achieved minor fame in the region for its musical accomplishments. After the early death of Raphael's mother, Josefina, the elder Baez placed their five-year-old son in school, where he began his musical education. Even early in his studies, Raphael exhibited a remarkable ability to recognize and transpose complex compositions. At the age of fourteen, he completed his studies at the College of Arts and Industries with high marks in arithmetic and composition and began his career as a professional musician in Mexico City. There he served as the assistant organist at the Metropolitan Cathedral for two years and then as a violinist with the Grand National Theater orchestra.

Baez seized an opportunity to expand his vistas in 1884 through the C. D. Hess Grand Opera Company. One of the many touring opera companies of the late nineteenth century traveling extensively throughout North America, it began a countrywide tour of Mexico in the spring of 1884. Arriving in Mexico City, company directors met Baez, who had begun to make a name for himself as a talented musician and promising composer. Baez joined the company in a tour of the main cities of Mexico throughout the rest of their time in the country. C. D. Hess identified in Baez a certain talent and panache. He invited the young *poblano* (Puebla native) to the United States at the close of the Mexican season to continue as the company's chorus master.

After completing his tour with the Hess Company in 1866, Baez settled in Milwaukee, where he accepted the position of organist and musical director at Gesu Church, one of the city's most prominent congregations. Outside of the church, his first major musical appearance in the city came at the twenty-fourth annual Säengerfest of the North American Säengerbund, at the Milwaukee Exposition Building in July

1886. The weeklong festival featured eighty-five music societies with more than twenty-five hundred singers performing. Baez played violin for a ninety-nine-member orchestra under the direction of renowned composer Ernest Catenheusen.

Baez continued to enjoy a successful career in Milwaukee. He served in several different positions in the city's churches and synagogues from 1886 to 1925, including organist and musical director at the Church of the Holy Name, organist at Holy Rosary Church, guest organist at Temple B'Ne-Jeshrun and Temple Emanu-El, full-time organist and director at St. John's Cathedral, and finally organist of St. Rose of Lima Church. Beyond his work as an organist and musical director, Baez also gained citywide prestige as a music teacher who stressed precision, punctuality, and practice. In 1887, Baez began teaching in his home, commencing a five-decade career that would make him one of the most sought-after music teachers in Milwaukee. The *Milwaukee Journal* referred to Baez as a "splendid coach" who, with even just a few musical lessons, was able to draw the "proper perception of the music" from his students." Baez taught piano, organ, and musical theory to students such as Hugo Goodwin, a concert organist who went on to become the organist and choir director of Chicago's St. Mark's Episcopal Church and New England Congregational Church, and Charles Hambitzer, who later became the piano teacher and principal musical influence of George Gershwin. After Baez spent years conducting private music lessons for the children of Milwaukee's elite, his acumen as an educator led him to a position as a music professor at Marquette College (now University) in 1892, making him the school's first Mexican faculty member. Baez also served as a language instructor for his university pupils, tutoring Marquette students in Spanish at his home.

Baez shared his dedication to music with his wife, Maria Catherine Schön, an accomplished vocalist and musician of German descent. The Baez duo, who were married on May 23, 1889, would often play together at musical performances, as they did for the Milwaukee Women's Club at the Athenaeum in 1904. They had four children, one of whom passed away as a baby. Raphael, the oldest son, served as an officer and squadron commander in the US Army Air Corps during World War II and later became a teacher in Bay View. His younger brother, Francis, served as an officer in the navy before returning to Milwaukee to work as a supervisor at Northwestern Mutual Life Insurance for more than thirty-five years. Their sister, Mary, also served her country on the home front at the navy's Bureau of Yards and Docks, after which she went on to work as the first Mexican American employee at the Milwaukee County Courthouse.

These early ambassadors from Mexico seem to have experienced little of the hardship of those who would follow. Formally educated and having acquired some material wealth, the Baezes were accepted into their adopted community and welcome to participate in civic and political activities. The young maestro donated his time and musical skills for charitable causes such as the St. Mary's Hospital benefit concert at the Pabst Theater in 1897, and he served on the Committee on Music for the leading Democratic Party organization in the state, the Jefferson Club. Baez also joined his fellow musicians in a number of musical organizations such as the Musician's Society of Milwaukee, and even helped establish melodic groups of his own, such as the Gounod Musical Club. His musical acumen was so well respected that firms such as the Puritan Phonograph Company sought out his endorsement for their products, which they glowingly included in advertisements for their phonographs in the city's newspapers. The statewide publication *Men of Progress* described Baez as a musician who had "built for himself an enviable place among the musical fraternity of his adopted home." By the time Raphael Baez passed away on May 20, 1931, some of his former compatriots had started to find their way to Wisconsin.

❦

WISCONSIN'S EARLIEST MEXICAN WORKERS

Although Baez found success and fame in Wisconsin, it was some time before other Mexicans followed. While experiences of later Mexican immigrants differed greatly from that of the famed musician, their core reason echoed his own: the search for a better life. Arriving for the most part after the settlement of most European-origin immigrants, Mexicans have striven to carve out their own space in Wisconsin and in its unique immigrant history. Unlike most other immigrant groups that historians have researched and chronicled, especially those groups from European countries that witnessed a sharp decline in immigration beginning in the 1920s, Mexican immigration to Wisconsin has continued and grown to the present day. Beginning with the arrival of the first large wave of agri-cultural and industrial workers in the early decades of the twentieth century, Wisconsin's Mexican community has grown to play an integral role in the state's cultural, social, economic, and religious history.

Accounts vary as to the first arrival and settlement of Mexican la-borers to Wisconsin, but reports place scattered groups at diverse parts of the state in the early twentieth century. In southwestern Wisconsin, more than thirty Mexican men were employed on the Chicago, Burling-ton, and Quincy (CB&Q) Railroad in the early 1910s. The men worked on the fence gang during the railroad's heyday, when the CB&Q stretched twelve thousand route miles in fourteen states across the Mid-west to Colorado, and down to the ports of Houston and Galveston. Living in Cassville, a Grant County village along the Mississippi River, the laborers worked and shopped at the town's C.J. Scharfenstein Gen-eral Merchandise Store.

Mexicans also began arriving in southeastern Wisconsin in the 1910s. In a speech delivered to the Professional Men's Club in 1926, noted com-munity leader William George Bruce stated that Mexicans had first ar-rived in Milwaukee in 1911. These early immigrants arrived to work in the city's tanneries, foundries, and factories. Many were *solteros*, or single men, who came to the city through work contracts.

While some Mexicans found work in cities, most early migrants to Wisconsin worked in the state's agricultural fields, many arriving by way of states in the US Southwest to work in the sugar beet industry. Called *betabeleros*, many of these workers filled positions that had been formerly held by Belgians and Russians as older waves of European immigrants moved on to family-owned farms throughout Wisconsin following World War I. Beet field owners sent labor recruiters into Mexico and the US Southwest in search of workers and paid the recruits' fare to Wisconsin. Employee contracts spelled out workers' yearly employment schedule, wages, and the number of acres they would work. Workers would arrive in Wisconsin around mid- to late April, many with their families, and would leave at the end of the harvest in late October after receiving their final wages. After fulfilling their contractual obligations, field owners would then pay for the Mexican families' return passage.

Changes in federal law drastically altered immigration patterns to Wisconsin in the years after World War I. The Emergency Quota Act of 1921, followed by the Immigration Act of 1924, placed a restrictive cap on the number of immigrants from southern and eastern Europe allowed entry into the United States. The quota acts severely constrained immigration from countries that had previously provided most new immigrants. But answering the demands of Southwest farmers for cheap, easily importable labor, federal legislators exempted the Western Hemisphere from the new limits. Because of Mexico's proximity to the United States, legislators believed that Mexican immigrants would make suitable guest workers who would come to the United States during peak labor periods such as planting and harvest seasons, and then return to their homes south of the border. Declining immigration from Europe also drove many Midwestern industrial employers, including Wisconsin companies, to turn to Mexico to meet rising labor needs in the first decades of the twentieth century. The recruitment of one Mexican worker typically led to a chain migration, as those who successfully secured employment sent word home of the availability of work and decent wages.

While some Mexican men made their way to Wisconsin in search of employment, others brought their families to the Midwest in the mid-1920s as political refugees. Brothers Juan and Francisco Sánchez recalled their parents' stories about the war-ravaged ranchos of Zacatecas, which had witnessed multiple clashes between the Federal Army and the revolutionary units led by Francisco "Pancho" Villa throughout the 1910s. Their father, Jesus Sánchez, had been fortunate enough to escape the drafting by Villa's army of able-bodied men during the revolution but counted himself most blessed to have escaped losing an ear as retribution for his refusal to enlist. The Sánchez brothers somberly recalled men walking the streets of Milwaukee's south side with only one ear, daily reminders of the turmoil they had left behind in Mexico. Fleeing the violence and economic disaster caused by the Mexican Revolution, families such as the Sánchezes found in Milwaukee stable work, a small Mexican community, and, most importantly, relative political peace.

By the mid-1920s, hundreds of thousands of Mexican immigrants replaced southern and eastern Europeans as the most heavily recruited immigrant workforce to the United States. Immigrants arriving directly from Mexico came from several states, including Guanajuato, Jalisco, Aguascalientes, Michoacán, Zacatecas, and Nuevo León. While most ended up working in fields or factories, the Mexicans who migrated to Wisconsin during this period came from a variety of class, educational, professional, and economic backgrounds. Some had been members of the professional class in Mexico, working in education, banking, engineering, medicine, civil service, or the arts. Others had served in the Mexican military during or after the Mexican Revolution. Mexican students enrolled at Marquette University, the Wisconsin State Teachers' College–Milwaukee (now the University of Wisconsin–Milwaukee), and the School of Engineering of Milwaukee (now the Milwaukee School of Engineering) to become lawyers, engineers, dentists, and physicians. Many returned to Mexico after completing their studies, disillusioned with the unwillingness of Wisconsin employers to hire them for anything but menial labor. Regardless of their educational level or past work experiences, the vast majority of the Mexican migrants and immigrants who arrived in Wisconsin found no such opportunities in the north, as nearly all were denied entry into higher-status jobs because of their race and instead shuttled into low-skilled and underpaying jobs in the dirtiest and least-respected sections of the city's industries.

One Mexican immigrant who came to Wisconsin in the early 1900s was Diego "Jimmy" Innes. Known as a musical prodigy in his native home of Oaxaca, Mexico, the young man came to the United States with the intention of continuing his musical education, first arriving in California in 1907. Despite his promising background, Innes worked in several jobs such as elevator operator and coffee wagon driver before finding work as a professional musician when he joined the Davidson Theater orchestra in Milwaukee in 1915. Over the next twenty-five years, he made a name for himself in the Milwaukee theater scene as a musician and conductor and played an important role in introducing Milwaukee residents to Latino music and culture. After becoming a US citizen in 1920, Innes helped bring twenty-five of his relatives from Mexico to the United States through a chain migration. Some eventually returned to Mexico after being unable to establish themselves in careers here.

Despite the limited opportunities available to them, many Mexican families stayed to give American life a chance, settling across Wisconsin in the first decades of the twentieth century. In Green Bay, the *Milwaukee Sentinel* reported on the first wedding between Mexicans in the city in 1920. Felipe Martins and Maria Ramirez had arrived the previous spring to work in the surrounding sugar beet fields and planned to make their permanent home in Green Bay after celebrating their nuptials. The newspaper reported with some interest that the newly married couple was breaking with recent tradition, as most Mexican farm laborers and their families returned home with the end of the harvest and the approach of winter. In Oshkosh, an eighteen-year-old youth, Alexander Hudson from Acapulco, enrolled at the local high school in 1930. Hudson had come to Wisconsin with his older brother, Alfred, who taught Spanish in night school classes. The *Sheboygan Press* reported that the young Alexander quickly learned English and enrolled in citizenship classes in anticipation of making Wisconsin his permanent home. And in Fond du Lac, where Mexicans first came to work in agriculture, a colony of twenty-five families had established homes and a small community by the early 1930s—one of many examples of Mexicans starting to form communities across the state.

Waukesha became home to one of Wisconsin's larger Mexican communities early on. Workers and their families came to labor in many industries in the growing town and its surrounding area, including International Harvester, Werra Aluminum Foundry, Quality Aluminum Casting Company, Waukesha Foundry, and General Castings Company. Most Mexicans settled in an area called The Strand, a neighborhood that was still predominately home to Italians throughout the 1910s and 1920s. The Melendes family, originally from Guanajuato, settled in 1919 in The Strand, where they operated a popular boardinghouse. Throughout Midwestern *colonias*, boardinghouses such as the one owned by the Melendes family became essential spaces for arriving immigrant Mexican workers. Not allowed to rent in residential sections, they found shelter and made connections at these friendlier establishments. Here single men could band together, find a place to lay their heads after a long day of work, and share a meal with their compatriots. Besides boarding homes, migrant workers who hoped to return to Mexico also found rustic accommodations in rooming houses such as the Commercial Hotel in Waukesha. By the early 1930s, the Mexican colony in Waukesha had grown to include around thirty families.

Many Mexicans who came to Wisconsin did not take a direct route from their home country. Porfirio Gonzalez from Sánchez, Zacatecas, originally left Mexico after signing a contract with the Santa Fe Railroad, where he paid eight dollars for his *papeles y visa* (papers and visa) to travel through Ciudad Juarez. While railroad work took many of his compatriots to California, Gonzalez ended up in Emporia, Kansas, where he laid railroad lines. Upset with the poor treatment and meager wages the company offered, Gonzalez left his position and made his way north in May

1927 to Chicago, where he found work in construction and laying sewer lines for the city's gas company. He eventually secured more stable employment in Milwaukee at the Greenbaum Tannery, where he worked until his retirement. Another eventual Milwaukee resident, Guadalupe "Lupe" Renteria, made the decision to immigrate to the United States after the death of his father. Originally from San Gaspar de los Reyes, Jalisco, Renteria traveled with his mother, Soledad, and brothers. The family passed through Texas en route to Iowa, where they worked and lived on a beet farm. After some time, the Renterias made their way to Joliet, Illinois, where an older sister had established a home. The young Lupe then ventured to Rockfield, Wisconsin, joining his brothers who worked on a railroad, before the family settled for good in Milwaukee in 1922. The search for steady work was often a driving factor, as it was for the optimistic Federico Herrera, who crossed into Laredo, Texas, in 1925. Herrera tried unsuccessfully to find work in Texas and Chicago before making his way to Milwaukee, where he hoped to "sweep up some of the gold off the streets" and "make [his] fortune," according to a *Milwaukee Journal* report.

Settlement in the United States and the pursuit of American citizenship were not necessarily the goal for all Mexican immigrants. Many saw their time in Wisconsin as temporary, intending to work for some months to save up money but to eventually return to their homes and families in Mexico. The particular case of Ismael A. Cárdenas, who moved to Milwaukee in the 1920s to find employment and leave the violence of the Mexican Revolution behind him, illustrates this longing to one day return to a native home. Cárdenas, the first cousin of Mexican president Lázaro Cárdenas, had served for ten years in the Mexican Army as a captain during the revolution, under the command of both his cousin Lázaro and General Francisco "Pancho" Villa. Turning down offers for promotion within the army, Cárdenas ventured to the American Midwest and found employment shoveling bull hides in the "wet department" of Milwaukee's Greenbaum Tannery. He went on to gain fame in Wisconsin as a wrestler of considerable skill, winning 110 light heavyweight bouts in Milwaukee under the name of Joe Fontaino. Cárdenas hoped to return to western Mexico, where he had left behind his wife and four children, to raise bananas and beans and perhaps even start his own tannery.

UNFRIENDLY RECEPTION IN MILWAUKEE

As Mexican workers began arriving in the first decades of the twentieth century, Wisconsinites debated if, and how, Mexicans would be integrated into their communities. Like Americans elsewhere, they deliberated whether the newest immigrants could be assimilated into existing culture, or if they should be excluded to protect national identity—a dilemma popularly referred to as "the Mexican problem" of the 1920s and 1930s. Even before the first migrants made their homes in Wisconsin, popular books and city newspapers disparagingly depicted Mexicans as being culturally and socially inferior. In a 1911 article, the *Milwaukee Sentinel* described Mexicans as "peons" who were "born in ignorance" and had been barely able to "eke out [a] bare existence" in their home country. According to reporters' accounts, the Mexican people were content with remaining illiterate and uneducated, lived in unsanitary conditions and were prone to disease, and didn't have the desire to pursue freedom. Referring to Mexicans as "gente sin razon" (people without reason), the *Sentinel* warned of intermingling with an "untrustworthy" civilization "born without virtue" and possessing "a defective mentality."

Other newspaper articles and reports prepared by city social workers portrayed Mexicans as dangerous criminals who were prone to idleness and drunkenness. These reports often relied on popular accounts and hearsay to cast doubts on the legal standing of Mexican immigrants in Milwaukee and throughout the country. The *Milwaukee Journal* warned that despite the legal barriers in place to restrict immigration, such as a literacy test, medical exam, and head tax, undocumented Mexicans were able to cross the loosely policed 1,800-mile-long border along the Rio Grande. The newspaper unscientifically estimated that legal entries equaled undocumented arrivals, a claim that could not be verified with information available at the time. Several editorials published from 1927 to 1930, the *Milwaukee Journal* advocated for extending the immigration quotas set on Europeans and Asians to Mexicans as well. A 1928 editorial stated that it was "ridiculous for us to leave the door from Europe only slightly ajar, if we are to leave the doors from the other countries of this hemisphere wide open." The newspaper's editors wrote that Mexican immigration was "above all a racial complication," as the hundreds of thousands of Mexican "peon laborers" and "half-breeds" entering the county were "entirely unassimilable." They further questioned whether Mexicans, who they called "if not full-blooded Indians, at least largely of Indian blood," were even eligible for American citizenship. According to immigration law at the time, only "free white persons and aliens of African nativity or persons of African descent" could apply for naturalization. The *Milwaukee Journal*'s editors believed—and hoped—this distinction would exclude Mexicans from eligibility for citizenship.

The widespread prejudice against Latino workers made life difficult for those trying to find their ways in a new life. Older European immigrants in particular carried resentment toward the newcomers, and at times the conflicts escalated to physical altercations. In one such encounter, Sandro Parris, a Mexican man who had arrived in Milwaukee in 1912, was reportedly involved in a brawl in his rooming house on the south side in 1916. Arriving home after a day of work, Parris encountered a group of European-origin roomers in the midst of a spirited discussion over the criminality of Mexican men. The discussion turned to the skirmishes between the US military and Mexican revolutionaries along the border region during the Mexican Revolution. The roomers' dismissive comments against Mexican revolutionaries angered Parris, and he challenged the men to a fight, a turn that ended with gunshots and police.

Such conflicts and difficulties mattered little to the Milwaukee companies that were determined to find cheaper and more readily controllable labor options. Employers avoided discussions of assimilability and citizenship as they continued to look south for new workers. Milwaukee's tanneries were among the first companies to recruit from Mexico. In the spring of 1920, the Pfister and Vogel Leather Company sent recruiters to Mexico in hopes of finding laborers to replace the company's unionized and striking workforce. The recruiters, known in Mexico as *enganchistas* (those who hook), promised Mexican men the opportunity to travel to the United States to find stable employment. The Mexican workers, many of them young, single men recruited from rural villages in the states of Michoacán and Jalisco, signed limited-term contracts. The *enganchistas* failed to mention, however, that many Mexican recruits would be used as strikebreakers. Being seen as taking the jobs of the city's unionized workers, making it harder for them to fight for fair wages and working conditions, did not ease the animosity between ethnic groups. The tannery placed its new workers in the Atlas warehouse on Virginia Street directly across from the tannery to protect them from striking laborers who wished to chase the newest immigrants out of the city. Milwaukee historian John Gurda observes that these initial living conditions were "not unlike those of a prison camp," as Mexican laborers toiled in their positions and lived in constant fear of violence.

Soon other Milwaukee companies followed the lead of Pfister and Vogel to save money on their labor forces. Plankinton Packing, the Bucyrus Company, the Harnischfeger Corporation, the Ladish Company, Allis Chalmers, England Steel, Northwestern Coke, Armour Meat Packing, the Milwaukee Road, and the Northwestern Railroads all began recruitment efforts in Mexico and the American Southwest in earnest in the 1920s. Mexicans who found themselves between jobs also worked on construction projects throughout the city, helping build the Schroeder Hotel and the Milwaukee County Court House.

As the threat of violence between striking workers and their Mexican replacements dissipated, newly arrived Mexicans settled in the neighborhoods that surrounded their workplaces, specifically on the near south side in Walker's Point, the Riverwest area, and Merrill Park. Their neighbors included the established ethnic communities of German and Polish immigrants as well as more recently arrived Bulgarians, Czechs, Greeks, Norwegians, Serbs, Slovenians, and Ukrainians.

🌿

COMMUNITY BUILDING IN THE *COLONIA*

As the number of Mexicans in Milwaukee grew, a loose *colonia*, or colony, developed as the city's newest immigrants created their own social and cultural institutions, becoming known as *los primeros*. Several entrepreneurs opened restaurants and grocery stores throughout the late 1920s and early 1930s. Arturo Morales, one of the first Pfister and Vogel recruits who had arrived in the early 1920s, managed to save and borrow the $2,150 he needed to open Milwaukee's first Mexican grocery in 1925. The Avila family also opened *La Companía Industrial Mexicana, Manufacturera y Importadora*, which served as a grocery and general store, restaurant, and manufactory and importing location for peppers and herbs, as well as kitchen goods like the *tamalina*, used to make tortillas, not usually found in the United States. The Avilas' restaurant served traditional Mexican dishes, like enchiladas, chiles (either canned or dried from Jalapa), and frijoles. Morales and the Avilas were later joined by Juan Robles, José Cárdenas, and Lucian Haro, who opened their own individual *tiendas* (stores) throughout the 1920s and early 1930s on the city's south side. Beyond providing cooking and home goods from the native country, grocers often also served as the community bank. Workers could deposit checks, either leaving the balance in an account or withdrawing it in cash.

The grocery stores provided Mexican families with small nourishing comforts that reminded them of home. Despite living thousands of miles away from their native country, many Mexican women continued to grind their own flour with a flat stone and a stone roller known as a metate to make the daily round of tortillas for their families. A *Milwaukee Journal* reporter, invited into a Mexican home in 1927, recounted the process:

> At one Mexican home, the senora was grinding flour on a stone. She knelt on the floor, the sloping stone in front of her, and rolled the grain with another stone, not unlike a rolling pin. This flour would be used for making tortillas—a staple Mexican dish—which take the place of our bread. At another home, the senora was baking tortillas, which are made fresh for every meal. In a large granite pan was the dough. She cut off bits of it and rolled them out very thin, making what looked like a pancake about eight inches in diameter. The top of the kitchen range was scoured clean. A hot fire had been built. The senora dropped the tortilla dough on the hot stove, waited until it was baked brown on one side, and with her fingers deftly turned it. When it was baked on both sides, she dropped it into a pan in which there were many more baked tortillas.

As they adjusted to life in Milwaukee, Mexican men and women came together throughout the 1920s and 1930s to create several social organizations. Like many of the European immigrants who had previously made their home in Milwaukee, Mexican community members created mutual aid societies, known as *mutualistas*. These organizations existed primarily to provide dedicated spaces to spend time with compatriots and to celebrate their shared cultural and ethnic identities, but they served more practical purposes as well. Through these organizations, more established Mexicans and community elders raised money to provide "starter funds," called *limosnas*, for newer arrivals. They also kept records, coordinating with the Mexican consulate in Chicago to more accurately report on the size of the growing community to better facilitate local consular services.

Two mutual aid societies dominated the Milwaukee Mexican social scene in the late 1920s and 1930s. La Sociedad Mutualista Hispano-Azteca, founded in 1929, began as a drama club that performed Spanish-language plays and musicals for the community. The organization El Círculo Social de Amigos "Emilio Carranza," founded later that year, sought to fill a similar artistic and social space. El Círculo Social was named in honor of the famed Mexican aviator Emilio Carranza, who had recently died in his attempt to fly from New York to Mexico City. The founders of these organizations included men who had received formal education in Mexico, such as José Pérez, who would go on to be a writer upon returning to Mexico in the early 1930s; Norberto Monares; and Miguel Sevilla Chávez, who had served as a professor in his native Michoacán.

These societies were also responsible for establishing the city's first Spanish-language newspapers, including *Sancho Panza* and *El Boletín Informativo*. Federico Herrera oversaw the publication of the first edition of *Sancho Panza*, the earliest Milwaukee Spanish-language newspaper, in July 1929. Printed on yellow paper the size of a handbill, the newspaper included "news stories, poetry, editorials, religious treatises, and patriotic exhortations" for the community. Regular editorials called upon members of the Mexican colony to "raise the level of Mexico to that of other civilized nations" by working toward citizenship and applying to the Mexican consulate for help when needed. Monthly columns also included the Department of Social Notes, which announced baptisms and births; "Voice of the Street," a section committed to opinions on current affairs, most of them religious; "Do You Know?" which offered interesting facts on cities from around the world; and the humorous "Seven Things That Make Me Laugh," which commented on the more light-hearted happenings that occurred among the city's Mexican residents. Due to limited finances and changing editorial teams, both *Sancho Panzo* and *El Boletín* had limited runs and ended publication in the early 1930s.

Mutual aid societies also took on the role of social functionaries, funding and hosting dances and celebrations for the city's Mexican community. Before the founding of the two societies, community members came together in an ad hoc manner to plan events, such as El Gran Baile (the Great Dance) of March 1927. Held at Harmonie Hall, the event was headlined by a performance by the Orquestra Chapultepec Jazz, and included the sale of traditional serapes, blanket-like shawls; Remington typewriters; and a free bottle of perfume for all women in attendance. The event was organized by Ismael Cárdenas, who coordinated advertising for the celebration through bilingual posters displayed throughout the city.

With the founding of groups such as La Sociedad Mutualista Hispano-Azteca and El Circulo Social de Amigos "Emilio Carranza," as well as later groups such as the Anahuac Dramatic Society, organizations could better coordinate and plan events around important Mexican holidays during the 1930s. The first Mexican Independence Day celebration was held on September 16, 1930, and included a parade through the Bay View neighborhood. The following year, directors from "Emilio Carranza" and Hispano-Azteca worked together to host a two-day celebration to commemorate the 121st anniversary of Mexican independence. Miguel Sevilla, president of "Emilio Carranza," recalled fondly the celebrations in his hometown of Michoacán, telling the *Milwaukee Journal*, "You should see it there. At 4 Tuesday morning, the band marches down the street, the church bells ring and every one comes out to start the fun. Races, bull fights, fireworks." The organizations hoped to capture at least a touch of the spirit of these revelries in their new homes in Milwaukee. The Milwaukee festivities began with an "Emilio Carranza"–organized celebration including dramatic and musical recitals and a dance at the south-side Turner Hall. Hispano-Azteca's festivities, held at Harmonie Hall the following day, began with a Catholic Mass in the morning followed by dancing in the evening. Speeches commemorated the memory of Don Miguel Hidalgo y Costilla, the "Mexican George Washington." Beyond Mexican Independence Day, the mutual aid organizations also celebrated Cinco de Mayo. This important Mexican holiday traditionally commemorates the anniversary of the victory achieved by the City of Puebla on May 5, 1852, by General Ignacio Zaragoza against the invading Expeditionary French Army. Hispano-Azteca and "Emilio Carranza" collaborated in 1933 for a two-day celebration of the military triumph. Organizers from the two societies came together under an umbrella organization they dubbed El Comité Patriótico (The Patriotic Committee), and then extended invitations to city officials, including

Mayor Daniel Hoan, and the larger community to share their cultural traditions with Milwaukeeans. Advertised through a bilingual poster, the event included civic, literary, musical, and dance components as well as "exquisite Mexican dinners." The city's Mexican Orchestra played a *paso doble* called "Sangre Morena," and children gave speeches on the importance of Cinco de Mayo. The festivities ended with the singing of the Mexican and US national anthems. The successful coordination of the 1933 event led these organizations to continue to work together to offer similar celebrations throughout the 1930s.

FINDING COMMUNITY THROUGH FAITH

Like many of the immigrant communities from Europe that preceded them, Mexican immigrant communities found that religious spaces served as central places for community formation and development. The majority of newly arriving Mexican immigrants were either Catholic or practiced many of the cultural traditions that defined the Mexican Catholic Church. For the workers and families that had traveled thousands of miles to Wisconsin to find work, the familiar religious experiences found in churches served as an escape from the difficult adjustment to a new life in the Midwest.

While racial animosities dominated relationships between Milwaukee Mexicans and members of other ethnic groups throughout the 1920s, religious spaces such as churches and lay organizations became sites of interethnic fraternity. Leaders within the European-origin Catholic community invited members of the expanding Mexican *colonia* into Milwaukee parishes in the mid-1920s, creating the beginnings of a community united under the banner of shared religious faith. With the aid of organizations such as the Knights of Columbus and the Society of Saint Vincent de Paul, the city's interethnic religious spaces became a welcome respite from the daily worries of backbreaking labor, cultural isolation, and racial discrimination.

Community leaders such as William C. Bruce and Frank Gross helped initiate much of the early outreach to Milwaukee's Mexican Catholic community through the Knights of Columbus. Throughout 1924 and 1925, a Knights committee worked to create connections to the city's newest immigrants by coordinating Spanish-language missions with the aid of a Mexican Jesuit priest working in Chicago. Mexican Catholics were moved to learn that a Spanish-speaking priest would deliver a Holy Mass, administer sacraments, and speak with them in their native language.

The Knights of Columbus also pushed to provide for the physical welfare of the city's Mexican community through collaboration with Catholic social organizations. The Knights' Frank Gross worked with the Society of Saint Vincent de Paul to supply the social services that Mexican families had been unable to access through the city's Department of Public Welfare. Gross called on Josephine Zimmerman, who worked in the central office of the Milwaukee branch of the society, and asked her to conduct home visits within the community to gather information on how best to serve the needs of the Mexican immigrants. The Spanish-speaking Zimmerman assisted Mexican immigrants in finding homes, employment, and food and helped families navigate the city's social welfare organizations. Mexican families came to trust Zimmerman, who actively listened to the community's concerns and advocated on their behalf whenever possible. These linguistic bridges were essential in creating connections between the European-origin and Mexican Catholic communities.

In May 1924, Milwaukee Mexican Catholics created the Mexican Committee, also known as El Club Mexicano, the first Mexican-led organization in the city. Like the Knights of Columbus, this organization served as a Catholic fraternal organization, hosting social events to foster community among parishioners. El Club held events throughout 1924, including community dances in collaboration with the Knights, who donated use of their meeting hall. Through these celebrations, the organization created the first spaces for Milwaukee Mexicans to celebrate their national heritage. El Club brought the community together to commemorate the Battle of Puebla in early May through prayer and dancing in an event sponsored by the Knights of Columbus. Advertisements for the event celebrated national pride with images that emphasized Aztec tradition and past military victories. The Battle of Puebla event marked the start of a celebration of traditional national festivals that lasted throughout the late 1920s and early 1930s.

Milwaukee Catholics, Mexican and European-origin alike, were brought even closer together with the outbreak of war in Mexico in 1926.

The hostilities that erupted between the Mexican state and Catholics in northern and western Mexico known as La Cristiada, or the Cristero War, captivated the city's Catholic press and spurred fund-raising efforts for the city's growing Mexican community. The *Catholic Herald* covered the state repression of the Church with weekly front-page updates, while the Knights of Columbus connected their efforts to assist Milwaukee's Mexican community with their greater project of defending the Catholic Church in Mexico. Religious leaders and elected representatives condemned the attack on religious freedom in a show of solidarity for Mexican Catholics living locally.

Catholic collaboration was also fundamental in the founding of the Mexican Mission chapel in 1926. Mexicans and the city's other Catholics worked together throughout the late 1920s to fund-raise for the purchase of a building and development of a new congregation. Milwaukee Catholics of all ethnicities were invited to attend the blessing of the Mexican Catholic community's new spiritual and social home in December 1926. They celebrated the dedication of the Mexican Mission Chapel of Our Lady of Guadalupe in accordance with the feast of the patroness saint of Mexico. In blessing the new chapel, Milwaukee Catholic archbishop Sebastian Messmer was joined by seven priests and deacons from Milwaukee parishes. With hundreds of Mexican congregants and other well-wishers in attendance for the dedication, some had to stand in the street to hear the blessing conducted by the archbishop.

The congregation gathered throughout the following years for a number of holiday celebrations, perhaps none more important than the novena held during the Christmas season. The nine-day observance of prayer began on Noche Buena, a day of great celebration that included the breaking of the piñata, an amusing figurine built around an earthenware container or paper bag and filled with nuts, sweets, and fruits. During the week of Christmas, the focus turned to the festival of Las Posadas, capped off with the performance of a dramatic play of the nativity called *Los Pastores* and the observance of the Day of Three Kings.

Religious spaces such as Our Lady of Guadalupe also served as matchmaking locations for romantic interethnic relationships, such as that between Margaret Cumming and Steve Pérez. Cumming met Pérez, who played the organ for the congregation, at the Mexican Mission in 1931, and the two quickly fell in love. Although interracial relationships were more common within Catholic congregations than elsewhere, couples such as this still faced obstacles to acceptance. Because of the interracial nature of their relationship, Cummings and Pérez had to meet clandestinely to avoid angering her parents, going to dance halls for two years before eloping in 1933. Alarmed to learn of the marriage, the woman's parents successfully petitioned a local judge for a warrant, resulting in the arrest of Pérez on a charge of "seduction." Luckily for the young lovers, both were of legal age at the time of marriage and could carry on with their lives after all charges were dismissed, albeit without the support of their families.

EDUCATION AND LANGUAGE BARRIERS

Learning a new language could be a challenge for newly arrived Mexican workers. In some cases, employers hoping to develop a more effective workforce provided English classes to their workers. The Menominee and Bay View plants of the Pfister and Vogel Leather Company offered English classes during breaks and after work hours three times a week, beginning as early as 1920. These courses offered rudimentary language skills for Mexican men to better navigate their jobs and understand their managers.

Language also provided a significant barrier for Mexican children trying to attend the city's public schools. The educational experience of Mexican children differed greatly from those of German and Polish students in the late nineteenth and early twentieth centuries. Germans and southern and eastern Europeans had successfully fought for public and parish schools to provide instruction in their native languages along with English. As a result, these immigrant groups were better able to learn in American schools while retaining their cultural and linguistic heritage. Milwaukee schools, which had a national reputation for their progressive language-immersion programs, did not extend the same recognition of language or culture to Mexican immigrants, as teachers saw their Spanish-speaking students as undereducated and uncultured. Teachers and administrators often criticized the city's newest immigrants for not doing more to integrate themselves into American society. The story of a young Mexican student in attendance at Vieau Elementary School demonstrates those difficulties. Like many Mexican children who came to Milwaukee in the 1920s, the student did not speak English and struggled to keep up with his American peers. His classroom teacher demanded that he return home until he learned English, at which point he would be allowed to rejoin his class. Because of such treatment, many Mexican students did not attend school or fell behind the educational achievement of their peers.

THE SPORTING LIFE

Language proved to be less of an issue in sports, which became a recreational outlet for many in the Mexican community. Baseball and softball were particularly popular among those who had played in their hometowns in Mexico. Federico Herrera, who had competed in leagues organized by mining companies in Mexico, joined informal games in the city's vacant lots. At one point Herrera joined a team consisting mostly of Germans, who gave him the nickname of "Fritz," an endearment that stuck with Federico for the rest of his life. As neither Herrera nor his teammates spoke much English, baseball became the universal language that brought his squad together. Throughout the late 1920s and early 1930s, Mexican community members played in a softball club called Los Amigos. With community interest high, players initially split themselves between two teams representing Our Lady of Guadalupe Church and played against teams from other Milwaukee parishes. Many active congregation members played for Los Amigos, including Juan Arenas; the Rios brothers, Enrique and Juan; Alfonso Najera and his brother Jesus, whom teammates called "Lefty"; Jorge Robles; Guadalupe "Lupe" Renteria; and Felix Renteria.

By the late 1930s, Los Amigos had gained enough playing time and experience to join the Northwest Kittenball Softball League, which was made up of teams from around the Milwaukee area. Announcing their entrance into the league in April 1938, the *Milwaukee Journal* noted that the all-Mexican team would add "a flash of color" for the upcoming season. The Mexican squad played its first game of the 1938 season against the league's defending champions, the Modern Furnitures, at the Vieau School playground. Los Amigos, composed of "fast, hardworking players," were managed by Guadalupe Renteria, a veteran of the first iteration of the team. Both teams brought their best hurlers to start the campaign, with Los Amigos calling on Enrique "Henry" Castillo, a senior at Milwaukee Boys Tech and basketball City Conference leading scorer, who promised to become a "pitching sensation." Beyond Castillo's pitching prowess, Los Amigos relied on the bat of "brilliant" first baseman Jubi Rodriguez, who gave the league's best pitchers a scare every time he stepped up to the plate. The *Milwaukee Journal* dubbed Los Amigos a "powerful contender" for the Northwest title thanks to the team's strong preseason play.

Young Mexican men also were drawn to boxing. Perhaps the most famous pugilist to arise from the community was Frank Grace, who had been recruited to Milwaukee by the promoter George Ryan in 1914. Billed as the "Milwaukee Mexican," Grace fought professionally for twenty years before retiring to train young Milwaukee Mexicans such as Federico Herrera throughout the 1920s and 1930s. Grace's retirement also included opening a popular pool hall in the area around Kinnickinnic and Lincoln Avenues. Pool halls such as Grace's became the center of recreation in the *colonia*, as Mexicans found themselves excluded from many of the city's public spaces, such as theaters and restaurants. The younger generation of boxers also included men such as Joe Ortez, known regionally as "Milwaukee's knockout king." Tutored by Bob Moha, a former middleweight star from Milwaukee, Ortez was described by the Milwaukee press as a "clever boxer" and "one of the hardest hitting bantams in the game."

THE GREAT DEPRESSION

Facing high unemployment with the onset of the Great Depression, Milwaukee's Mexican colony shrank considerably during the 1930s. In 1933, only a quarter of all wage earners in Milwaukee still had a job, while one of every five families was on some form of public aid. Because Milwaukee businesses viewed Mexican workers as surplus labor, they were usually among the first employees laid off from the city's factories and tanneries. Felix González remembered in a 1975 interview that a large majority of the single men who had come to Milwaukee in search of work returned to Mexico in the early years of the Depression, while many families were forced to stay due to high travel costs. In some cases, relief agencies or county governments paid the fares for those who wanted to return home, a practice that helped relieve the growing strain on public welfare cases. By 1933, the Mexican community in Milwaukee had fallen to fewer than 1,500 residents. Organizations such as the Society of St. Vincent de Paul and the Family Welfare Association did their best to provide welfare aid and employment opportunities for struggling Mexican families throughout the 1930s.

Depleted county welfare resources and rising anti-immigrant sentiment fueled crackdowns on undocumented immigrants throughout the Great Depression. Local elected officials collaborated with federal immigration officers, such as Milwaukee's chief immigration officer, Herman R. Landon, to search for immigrants on the county's welfare rolls. Undocumented or not, many of these individuals would be apprehended and then taken for deportation proceedings in Chicago. Federal immigration policy officially listed numerous causes for deportation proceedings, including illegal entry (which included overstaying a visitor's permit or crossing the border after giving false information or avoiding inspection), receiving public assistance within five years after entry, being a member of "immoral causes," and crime involving "moral turpitude." In practice, Mexicans of any documentation status could be deported after having been accused of committing even the most minor of crimes.

Across smaller Mexican communities in Wisconsin, local officials and welfare boards hoping to reserve county resources initiated deportation proceedings by accusing Mexicans of abusing county resources. In 1932, Racine's county treasurer and humane agent, searching for abuses after suspecting Mexicans of begging in surrounding towns, successfully pushed for the deportation of a Mexican family of eight working in the sugar beet fields near Union Grove. The official disregarded the unlikelihood that the employed family had been among the supposed beggars. These officials justified their actions to the city's press by arguing that sending Mexicans out of Wisconsin would help save the county money in the long run. In Fond du Lac, a Mexican man, who had arrived in Wisconsin in search of employment in 1923, was accused of having swum across the Rio Grande two years prior. The *Milwaukee Journal*, in spite of the impossibility of the alleged timeline, mockingly noted that the Mexican national had supposedly arrived in the United States without documentation and with barely any worldly possessions, but would now be deported "in style" with "plenty of luggage, and riding the cushions of a fast train." A young La Crosse resident and railroad worker was similarly accused of undocumented entry into the country via the Rio Grande before being pressed into deportation proceedings in 1935.

Deportation cases often divided families, especially when fathers were deported and mothers and children were left behind. The *Milwaukee Journal* reported such a case in 1931, as a Mexican mother with eight children, all but two born in the United States, faced the prospect of providing for her family on her own after her husband was deported on charges of being in "ill health." Despite having lived in the United States for thirteen years, the mother, who had no employment at the time of her husband's deportation, was denied any state aid for her family.

Beginning in 1930, the editorial board of the *Milwaukee Journal* advocated for stricter enforcement of border security to prevent the crossing of Mexicans into the United States. At a minimum, the board demanded that immigration officials properly categorize Mexican immigrants with regard to their racial identity. Instead of classifying them as white, which allowed for unfettered entry into the United States, the board insisted border officials invoke aspects of immigration law that "excluded every Mexican of Indian blood" from entry into the country, as this specific immigrant had proven "so difficult to assimilate in this country."

WORLD WAR II

While the Mexican community remained relatively small in the years following the Great Depression, Mexicans in Wisconsin joined the millions of Americans who supported the nation's efforts during World War II. Nationally, more than 500,000 Latinos, including more than 350,000 Mexican Americans, served in the US Army, Navy, and Marine Corps, in all theaters of battle. Many young Wisconsin Mexican Americans registered or were drafted to serve their home or adopted country during the war. Ray Bacalzo, a Milwaukee resident whose family was part of *los primeros*, recalls that when the war began, his neighborhood in Milwaukee "just about emptied out. All the guys, the young men, they went off to war." Even young men of Mexican descent who weren't American citizens attempted to register to join the war effort. In 1941, twenty-seven-year-old Antonio C. Uribe, who was studying radio engineering in Green Bay on scholarship through the Mexican government, applied for selective service. As a Mexican citizen, however, Uribe was deemed ineligible for the US armed forces by Mexican consular services.

The soldiers of Mexican descent performed admirably, many receiving commendations and some even giving their lives. David Valdes Jr.'s family had moved to Milwaukee from Michoacán in the late 1920s. An all-star basketball player for Milwaukee Boys Tech High School, Valdes entered the army air force in 1941. The twenty-one-year-old gunner was killed in action in 1944 when the B-24 Liberator on which he served was shot down over Hungary. Another Milwaukee resident, Ricardo "Chico" Ogas, who served in the US Navy as an electronic technician aboard the USS *Honolulu*, fought in the Pacific Theater and was involved in the Battle of Guadalcanal, where he was awarded multiple honors including eight Bronze Stars. The Enriquez brothers of Milwaukee, whose father owned the Viva Jalisco restaurant on Florida Street, served in Iceland and Greenland. Throughout the war, both brothers wrote home with longing for their mother's tamales, fried pinto beans, and *fideo* (fried string noodles).

The young soldiers received support from their families back in Wisconsin. Members of the growing Mexican community on Milwaukee's south side organized the Mexican Victory Club in 1943 to look after the welfare of the young Mexican-descent men of the colony who were serving with the United States armed forces. The club hosted a number of dances and picnics throughout the war to send five dollars cash to each of the eighty-five Mexican men in service. The original community leaders of the Victory Club included president Baudel Rodriguez, vice president Francisco Guerra, secretary Juan Santos Herrera, and vice secretary Hortencia Hernandez. The community also provided spiritual support for the soldiers, as families would gather weekly to light votive candles and pray for the safe return of their fathers, sons, and brothers at the Our Lady of Guadalupe parish.

Mexicans and Mexican Americans joined in the rapid expansion of industrial work to support the war effort on the home front as well. Throughout the war, companies such as Waukesha's General Malleable Corporation, producer of castings for war production, added workers of Mexican descent, most originally from Texas. General Malleable's personnel manager, Phil Olson, toured northern Wisconsin to recruit

Mexican workers and then helped settle them in Waukesha for their temporary employment. The Mexican laborers worked through the winter season and then returned to the beet fields in spring.

Upon returning from war, some soldiers of Mexican descent found that their language skills and experience in Latin American communities were now seen as useful skills by area employers. In December 1944, Leo García, who had trained as a paratrooper at Fort Benning, Georgia, returned to Milwaukee after his tour of duty. Because he was bilingual, García was an attractive candidate for companies looking to expand their markets into Latin America. The lithography firm Dosie & Johnson hired the former artist as an apprentice, with hopes that García would serve as a connector for future business interests in Spanish-speaking nations.

In April 1947, members of Milwaukee's veterans community formed the state's first Mexican American veterans' organization through the Catholic War Veterans. Based out of the Our Lady of Guadalupe parish, Post 1279 began with thirty-four members and parish pastor Michael Brown as the group's chaplain. Post 1279 was active in the Mexican American community throughout the 1940s. The veterans even formed a softball team, and took home the Catholic War Veterans league title in 1947. When the state organization hosted a parade in July 1949 for all soldiers fallen during World War II, members of the growing *colonia* also played a prominent role. The march included the commemoration of four Mexican American soldiers from Milwaukee who had died in the war: Hector Cervantes, David Valdes Jr., Salvador Flores, and Arturo Quiroz.

❧❧

POSTWAR COMMUNITY LIFE IN
THE MILWAUKEE AREA

Milwaukee's Mexican community, decimated by the economic depression of the 1930s, came to life again in the years following World War II. Reports estimated that between 2,500 and 3,000 Mexicans lived in southeast Wisconsin in the mid- to late 1940s. In 1950, University of Wisconsin–Milwaukee sociology student Salvador Valdovinos, in consultation with Angel Gutierrez, the former president of La Sociedad Mutualista Hispano-Azteca, conducted a door-by-door survey of the Mexican *barrio*.

They identified about 350 families, or about 1,750 people of "Latin descent," living within the limits of the city alone. The Mexican community in the Milwaukee metropolitan area would continue to grow in subsequent years as immigrants and migrants moved to the city for better-paying work.

As they had in the 1920s, Mexican immigrants to Milwaukee looked to establish a social life outside of their work. La Sociedad Mutualista Hispano-Azteca, founded at the end of the 1920s, served as the base for many community organization initiatives throughout the middle of the twentieth century. Paying members to the mutual aid society had access to life and death benefits and helped organize social events such as picnics, dances, and patriotic festivals. The organization served as the host for many of the Milwaukee Mexican community's cultural events throughout the 1940s and 1950s. Swinging occasions such as the June 1944 dance at Harmonie Hall, which included live jitterbug music and a feast of enchiladas, served as welcome breaks from long workdays. A picnic in 1949 on the city's south side drew more than 1,500 community members, as well as Mayor Frank Zeidler. After helping open the day's baseball game, Zeidler, quoted in *El Mutualista*, told the crowd, "All of us are brothers, all of us are equal, all of us are Americans."

Cinco de Mayo and Mexican Independence Day celebrations continued to headline community events through the period. The 1946 Independence Day festivities featured young Ignacio "Nacho" Zaragoza, known in the community as "el joven charrito" (the young cowboy), who sang popular Mexican songs while children twirled in traditional dances like *el jarabe*. The day's event culminated in the performance of *El Grito de Libertad*, a patriotic play composed by community leader David Valdes Sr. The 1948 Cinco de Mayo fiesta, which featured poetry, dancing, singing, and a cultural homage at Armory Hall, drew visitors from nearby Waukesha and Racine. The following year, the Cinco de Mayo festivities grew to include a parade of thirty cars led by two *charros* (cowboys) in full regalia on horseback down Milwaukee's near south side. Mayor Zeidler and other elected officials attended as invited guests and enjoyed musical stylings provided by a Mexican orchestra.

Mexicans also flocked to cities surrounding Milwaukee with rising opportunities in industrial jobs. With these growing communities came new organizations, such as El Club Mexicano Cuauhtemoc de Racine and La Sociedad Mutualista Mexicana de Waukesha. Mexicans from

Kenosha, Racine, Waukegan, and Milwaukee gathered in Racine in September 1948 to celebrate the city's first Mexican Independence Day festival. With Racine County officials and Mexican consular representatives in attendance, revelers at Memorial Hall watched a civic program, enjoyed songs performed by a children's choir, and danced the night away to music provided by a Mexican orchestra recruited from Chicago.

Hispano-Azteca also worked to unite Mexicans in Milwaukee with those who lived in surrounding towns. The mutual aid society's efforts to coordinate with other Mexican organizations in the region—such as La Sociedad Mutualista Mexicana de Waukesha, El Club Mexicano Cuauhtemoc de Racine, and La Sociedad Mexicana de Waukegan—culminated in the formation in 1950 of Las Sociedades Mexicanas del Medio-Oeste (the Mexican Societies of the Midwest). Beyond sharing resources for community celebrations, the committee fought back against those sowing hate and carrying prejudice against people the Mexican community and those who objected to the very presence of Mexicans in the region.

In the early 1940s, young Mexicans also formed organizations to celebrate heritage music and dancing. The most popular of these, El Club Estrellita, was a youth organization founded to learn and perform native Mexican dances and songs. Wearing traditional Mexican costumes, members performed at public community events such as the breaking of the piñata during the *posada* celebration—a Christmas festival—at Vieau School. In December 1941, the Milwaukee school's twelfth annual *posada* drew more than two hundred partiers. The *Milwaukee Journal* reported that the "corridors [were] alive" with children wearing "red and green and black costumes that sparkled with brilliants." Those in attendance were able to watch a movie brought to Milwaukee from Mexico, prompting the audience to "clap and yell with delight" as scenes of their homeland flashed across the screen. The night culminated with the breaking of the piñata, as children scattered to collect the fifty pounds of candy that dispersed with the decorated figure's shattering.

Wisconsin's Mexican community also relished their access to locally produced periodicals. While readers had turned to Spanish-language press from other states over the preceding two decades (such as Chicago's *The ABC* and Texas's *La Prensa*), La Sociedad Mutualista Hispano-Azteca's monthly newspaper, *El Mutualista*, became the state's most popular Spanish periodical, with its inaugural issue printed in September 1947. The newspaper's editors published information about important religious events such as baptisms, first communions, and weddings. Its pages also were filled with stories about Milwaukee Mexicans' sojourns back to their home country, varied odes to Mexico through prose and poetry, and articles on Mexican and American cultural exchanges happening in neighborhoods. In a column on the Anglicization of the Spanish language, a writer bemoaned the new slang spoken by many second-generation Mexican Americans, who used such phonetic conversions as *beisment* for basement (instead of *sótano*), *bos* for bus (instead of *camión*), and *dauntaun* for downtown (instead of *centro*). The paper also was a source of work advertisements, especially when farmers outside of Milwaukee sought seasonal agricultural laborers. *El Mutualista* also tracked Milwaukee's growing Latin music scene throughout the postwar years. One of the most popular acts, José Martinez and his Latin American Orchestra, specialized in rhumbas, sambas, boleros, tangos, and guaraches. Throughout the 1940s and 1950s, the band performed nightly at places such as Tex Strauss's Club Sienna in West Allis, the Continental Theater on National Avenue, and Club 26 on North Avenue. Martinez, who played clarinet and saxophone, had first started the band in Mexico in 1936. Martinez learned a variety of music styles, from Texas polkas to tropical cha-chas and rhumbas, as a migrant worker in the American Southwest. The musician settled in Milwaukee during World War II, where he found work in a tannery, and organized one of the first Milwaukee-based Latin orchestras. Thanks to his early work in growing the city's Spanish-language music scene, Martinez is now revered as one of the fathers of Latin music in Milwaukee.

Beyond live music, Spanish speakers could also tune their radios to hear Latin music and updates on current events beginning in the late 1940s, thanks to the work of Dante Navarro. Born in Mexico City in 1919, Navarro came to the Milwaukee area in 1948 by way of Chicago, settling in Cudahy and working as a hydraulic press operator for the Ladish Company. In 1949, Navarro started Wisconsin's first Spanish-language radio program, "The Spanish Radio Hour," on radio station WUFX. Navarro helped create bilingual radio programs throughout southeastern Wisconsin in the following decades, including a weekly spot on Racine's WRAC called Spanish Radio of Racine. He eventually produced the first daily radio program in Spanish on radio station WQFM in 1972. Navarro would eventually run for public office in Milwaukee in 1970, unsuccessfully vying to be the assemblyman for the Twelfth Ward but in the process becoming the first Latino in Wisconsin to seek an elected political position.

Milwaukee Mexicans also had access to a growing number of Mexican restaurants and grocery stores in the city throughout the 1940s and 1950s. José Cárdenas's store on Sixth and Walker Streets, and the city's oldest Mexican store, owned by Arturo Morales, on Fifth Street and Florida Avenue, continued to offer patrons chiles, traditional candies, and other imported foods from their home country. As Milwaukee's Mexican community grew, new restaurants sprang up throughout the city's south side. At El Canario Amarillo on North Water Street, proprietor Loreto Valdes offered traditional Mexican dishes. La Perla on South Sixth Street, a *tortilleria* (tortilla maker) and *panaderia* (bakery), offered fresh Mexican sweet breads and imported Mexican goods. As Mexican cuisine grew in popularity among Americans, the *Milwaukee Journal* offered a tour of the Mexican restaurants of Milwaukee in a special feature in 1944. The tour began with Juan Enriquez's restaurant, Viva Jalisco, on West Florida Street, named after Enriquez's native state. At Viva Jalisco, which included a small dining area with two tables and five counter stools, Juan's wife, Gregoria, wielded the frying pan and chile peppers, while daughter Juanita used the large *molino* (pulverizing machine) to grind the white corn for the fresh, daily tortillas. Gregoria used the tortillas to make enchiladas, which the *Milwaukee Journal* described as "a mixture of green chili sauce, grated cheese, ground fried pork, onions, and peppers." The newspaper's tour continued on to La Paloma on North Water Street. Owned by Mauro Torres, who called his cuisine a Spanish-Mexican mix, La Paloma featured huevos rancheros, fresh avocados, and a specialty dish called "pigs feet Mexicana." While enjoying their meal, patrons could listen to love ballads in Spanish played on the restaurant's jukebox. For those readers adventurous enough to try their hand at making Mexican cuisine at home, the article concluded with recipes for frijoles con chili and chili con carne.

GROWING CONGREGATIONS
IN MILWAUKEE AND BEYOND

The rebirth of the city's Mexican community after the war brought a revival in the activities of the Catholic Mission Chapel. In September 1944 the Milwaukee Catholic Archdiocese purchased the Old Hanover Exchange building, the former home of the Wisconsin Telephone Company on West Washington and Third Streets, to accommodate the growing congregation at Our Lady of Guadalupe. The congregants hoped to use the expanded space for a social center for the affiliated three hundred families. The growing congregation also prompted archdiocesan officials to recognize Our Lady of Guadalupe as a full parish in May 1946. Organizations affiliated with the Mexican parish used the larger space to host a number of religious and community celebrations during the 1940s and 1950s. They also held events throughout the neighborhood, such as a Mexican bazaar at the South Side Armory Hall in August 1945. While the main feature of the event was traditional food, with a menu including tamales, enchiladas, and tostadas, attendees were also treated to the musical offerings of Los Trovadores del Sur, an orchestra from Mexico City.

Other southeastern communities also saw the development of religious congregations within Mexican communities. In 1956, Racine's Catholic Dominican College invited more than five hundred Mexican-descent families from the area for the annual *posada*. College faculty and students organized the event in cooperation with the St. Vincent de Paul Society. Under the direction of spiritual leader Monsignor Henry Schmitt, the society also directed the construction of a chapel that served as the place of worship and community center for Mexicans living in the Sheridan Woods area of Racine.

By the early 1950s, religious denominations besides the Catholic Church also began to engage in outreach efforts to the state's Spanish speakers. In 1952, the Wisconsin Baptist State convention recruited Reverend Eleucadio Mendez, born in Mexico, to administer to the state's growing Mexican and Puerto Rican communities. Mendez estimated that at least 25 percent of the community was nominally Protestant, but many belonged to no church. In Milwaukee, members of the new Spanish-speaking Baptist Church moved their services to the former site

of the Ebenezer Evangelical Free Church on South Seventh Street after
outgrowing their temporary home at the Christian Center on Washington Street. In July 1957, the Spanish Speaking Baptist Church hosted two
hundred delegates from ten states in the Midwest for the North Central
Area conference of the Spanish-American Baptist Convention.

MAKING TIME FOR SPORTS

By the mid-1940s, sports and recreation in the Mexican community
began to expand beyond softball and baseball. Fans of wrestling could
root for *lucha libre* (professional wrestling) stars who passed through Milwaukee's wrestling circuit. With colorful names such as "Don
Moctezuma" and "The Mexican Cry Baby" (the moniker of Miguelo
Torres), these grapplers wowed crowds of all ages with matches at the
South Side Armory Hall and Bahn Frei Hall.

Throughout the 1940s, Mexican youth laid claim to city and state
titles in the competitive field of marbles known as mibs. Mexican youth
Vitensio Prado reigned as the Milwaukee city marbles champion for six
years. Beginning his run at the age of eight, Prado, known as the "little
Mexican mibs marksman," was considered one of Wisconsin's leading
players. A student at Vieau School, Prado represented the city of Milwaukee at state tournament after state tournament, placing as a runner-
up in 1945 and finally claiming the state champion title in 1947.

Mexican men also jumped on a growing national craze of bowling.
Avid bowlers formed Milwaukee's first all-Mexican bowling team in May
1946. That year, a team captained by Guadalupe Renteria and sponsored
by the Frank and Catherine Taverns finished fourth in the Teutonia 800
league. In 1948, the same crew matched up against another Mexican
team from Fond du Lac, led by brothers Rafael and Jesús Ruiz. In the
1950s, Mexican bowlers sponsored by the Mexico Inn successfully pres-
sured the American Bowling Congress, formerly an exclusively all-white
male organization, for entrance into the annual championship tournament.

FIGHTING FOR A PLACE IN AMERICA

As first-generation immigrants came to establish families throughout Wisconsin, Mexicans and Mexican Americans grappled with their national and ethnic identity and questions of integration throughout the late 1940s and 1950s. Milwaukee resident Gladys Valdovinos discussed the difficulty of navigating these questions in responding to a *Milwaukee Journal* article decrying the rise of the "hyphenated American" in the postwar years. Valdovinos began by claiming her rightful place as an American, stating that her ancestors had settled in the United States before the start of the American Revolution. Her husband, Salvador, who had recently become a citizen after fighting for the United States during World War II, also "certainly appreciated his citizenship more than those of us who were born here and take the advantages of citizenship for granted." While the couple planned to raise their children "to be proud of their American heritage," they also intended to give them every opportunity to know and love their father's birthplace, Mexico. The children would grow up in America but would also be exposed to their Mexican heritage through Milwaukee's Mexican colony and the customs they were helping preserve. Valdovinos finished her letter with a call for tolerance and acceptance: "Where I feel we Americans do fail, however, is that so few of us appreciate or even tolerate the beauty of the customs of nationality and racial groups other than our own. A little more tolerance and willingness to give the other guy a chance is what we need."

A number of Wisconsin Mexicans joined national organizations throughout the period focused on civil rights and questions of integration and assimilation. In 1957, community members in Milwaukee, Waukesha, Kenosha, and Racine formed separate chapters of the League of United Latin American Citizens (LULAC). Founded in Texas in 1929 in protest of discrimination against people of Latin descent, LULAC to this day advocates for citizenship education that will foster better relations between citizens of Mexican descent and other Americans. In June 1957, the Racine LULAC chapter hosted a regional convention at Memorial Hall. Wisconsin governor Vernon W. Thomson and Racine mayor Jack Humble issued proclamations designating June 15–22 as LULAC Week in honor of the league's work. Governor Thomson served as the keynote banquet speaker, stating that Wisconsin was "grateful to the Latin Americans for the culture and tradition which they have added to this state" and that persons of Latin American descent would surely lend "strength and beauty" to Wisconsin. Attendees to the banquet included Mayor Humble, Milwaukee mayor Frank Zeidler, national LULAC president Felix Tijerina, and envoys from LULAC chapters in Illinois, Iowa, and Indiana. More than six hundred delegates were also in attendance from all parts of the United States, as well as invited guests from Costa Rica, Colombia, Peru, and Venezuela.

In the years following World War II, more and more Mexicans and Mexican Americans also entered leadership positions in organized labor. Guadalupe Renteria, serving at the time as the secretary of Hispano-Azteca, was elected by his coworkers as the shop chairman at the Trostel Tannery in 1948. *El Mutualista* reported that Renteria's election marked the first time a Mexican had achieved the position of a "labor leader" in the city. In spring 1948, editors of *El Mutualista* also covered the elections of Locals 47 and 260 of the Fur and Leather Workers of the United States and Canada held throughout Milwaukee tanneries where many Mexicans worked, such as Trostel, Greenbaum North Side, Greenbaum Bay View, Abel & Bach, and Wisconsin Leather. Mexican candidates for union positions in 1948 included Guadalupe Renteria, hoping to be elected as a delegate to the International Convention; Gilberto Valdes, vying for a spot on his local's executive board; and Arturo Manríquez and Federico Herrera, both nominees for trustees positions.

LOS BRACEROS

America's entry into World War II heralded a dramatic shift in industrial and agricultural production to help support the growing war effort. With higher-paying jobs available in urban centers, rural Wisconsin witnessed a demographic shift in the 1940s. From 1940 to 1946, approximately 140,000 people migrated from rural areas to Wisconsin's cities, as many workers left their farms to seek industrial jobs. Rural farmers also struggled to compensate for the loss of young, able-bodied workers to the draft. With men leaving to serve in the armed forces, Wisconsin's 186,000 farmers were called on to harvest more crops with less manpower on hand to work the fields.

The wartime Wisconsin labor dilemma was part of a larger national manpower shortage. Political leaders in Washington turned to immigration from Mexico and the Caribbean throughout the 1940s to supplement the needed labor. They forged several agreements, including the 1942 Mexican Farm Labor Agreement and the national Emergency Farm Labor Program initiated in 1943. These pacts allowed for coordination between federal agencies such as the State Department, the Department of Labor, Immigration and Naturalization Services, and state offices for the recruitment of agricultural workers. In Wisconsin, these agreements allowed farmers to enlist male workers from Mexico, Jamaica, the Bahamas, and British Honduras (present-day Belize), as well as prisoners of war from Germany and Italy, to work primarily in the harvest of sugar beets and cherries, as well as pea and corn canneries. The total number of foreign guest workers in Wisconsin grew from 1,300 in 1943 to 3,000 in 1944, 3,200 in 1945, and 3,600 in 1946. The number then fell to 2,800 in 1947 in the final year of the first Mexican Farm Labor Agreement Program.

The 1942 Mexican Farm Labor Agreement, also known as the Bracero Program, was the first in a series of guest worker programs initiated by the United States and Mexican governments. *Braceros* (derived from the term *brazo*, or arm) were Mexican manual laborers hired on limited contracts to work in the United States. The initial iteration of agreements lasted from 1942 to 1947 and were followed by a series of labor pacts that lasted until 1964. Between 1942 and 1964, the United States admitted more than 4.6 million workers under the Bracero Agreement, the majority of whom worked in southwestern and Pacific Coast states.

Hoping to avoid many of the abuses and the "starvation wages" that had befallen migrant workers in the previous four decades, the Mexican government entered into direct negotiations with the US government, instead of with employers. Under the negotiated terms, Mexican migrants were guaranteed season-long positions, would be compensated at the local minimum wage, and would have their transport and food paid while en route to their worksite and back to Mexico at the end of the season. The US government also promised to extend the same benefits to Mexican workers with regard to housing, sanitation, workplace safety, and medical attention as were available for citizen workers.

Despite these explicit contractual protections, *braceros* arriving in states such as Wisconsin quickly found themselves in precarious living and working conditions. Farm laborers arrived each April by railway car to Chicago, where, because of the constant movement of soldiers and supplies headed out to war, they waited for days on train station platforms with irregular access to meals and no proper shelter. When they eventually arrived at the farms that would employ them throughout central Wisconsin, promises of proper compensation, decent housing, and sanitary facilities went largely unmet. Instead of finding adequate living quarters, Mexican workers on farms across the state lived in repurposed boxcars with poor ventilation and inadequate restrooms. Laborers received unreliable and inadequate medical care, as company doctors who did not speak Spanish slackened the standards for medical examinations. Serious illnesses such as bronchial pneumonia were sometimes purposefully misdiagnosed as "bad colds" so employers could avoid providing proper care or sending ill workers back to Mexico. In addition, Mexican workers received little in the way of occupational safety protections and workmen's compensation. Painful, debilitating injuries suffered in the fields were met with indifference from employers. Some Mexican guest workers, angry with the working and living conditions they found in Wisconsin, voiced their displeasure with their feet by abandoning their worksites and their contracts early. Known as "quits," they then made their way to larger urban centers such as Milwaukee in search of higher-paying work in factories or foundries. Many had been mechanics or drivers in Mexico and preferred higher-paying industrial labor to agricultural work.

In an effort to protect its citizens working in the United States, the Mexican government embargoed states that failed to hold offending employers accountable. The Mexican government sanctioned Wisconsin—along with Texas, Colorado, Illinois, Indiana, Michigan, Minnesota, Montana, and Wyoming—multiple times throughout the 1940s because of both working conditions and social circumstances in receiving towns and communities. Reverend Ellis Mashburn, Midwest migrant supervisor of the Home Missions Council of North America, described some of their experiences to the *Milwaukee Journal* in 1949. Migrant workers did not like to work in Wisconsin because of "mistreatment in retail stores" and restaurants, as well as "social rejection and general attitude of unfriendliness with which they meet at the hands of the nonagricultural residents" in the communities in which they worked, he reported.

Despite these deplorable conditions, *braceros* played an especially important role in the Door County cherry harvests throughout the war.

Thousands of Mexican workers passed through the region in the 1940s, most hailing from Mexico City, Michoacán, and Guanajuato. These workers were crucial in overcoming the burden of wartime labor shortages and machinery. In 1944 alone, the seven million pounds of cherries Mexican hands helped harvest went directly to military procurement agencies for distribution to the armed forces overseas. *Braceros* worked across sixty-seven camps and four processing plants, oftentimes alongside migrant workers from the Caribbean, prisoners of war, and even troops of young Boy Scouts recruited to lend a hand. The work was deemed crucial enough that an attaché of the Mexican consulate was on site to inspect the orchards and straighten out any wage issues immediately, a stipulation that at times helped Mexican workers but often failed to address all of their working and living concerns.

While the majority of Mexican guest workers were sent to work in the agricultural industry, a small number also worked in Milwaukee's railroad shops. More than one hundred underdressed, shivering young Mexican men were first dropped off at the road shops in the Menominee River Valley on a cold February day in 1944. Stationed in the shadows of the Thirty-Fifth Street viaduct, the workers were crammed into two former storage buildings that had been converted into dormitories. Contracted to work for six-month periods, the *braceros* sent most of their money home to their families, as 70 percent of the young men were married. The workers stated that, aside from the opportunity to work, they came to the United States "to see the country, to get the experience in the shops or maybe to learn some English." By 1945, the railroad crew had grown to more than 180 workers.

The *braceros* did their best to create a sense of community in the railroad colony. As only a half dozen of the men spoke English, the workers relied on their informal leader, Juan Gonzáles, who served as interpreter and a company liaison. Men did their own washing at an on-site laundry and set up a makeshift barbershop run by Pedro Ramirez, known to his comrades as the "Mexican Figaro." The men also constructed a recreation room where resting workers could listen to the radio, practice their guitars, join in song, or write letters home to their loved ones. After petitioning their employers for more educational and recreational activities, the workers seized the opportunity to learn English and more about the United States through night classes offered by the Milwaukee Public Schools Department of Adult Education and the Milwaukee County

Municipal Recreation Department. *Braceros* attended classes in a red-painted recreation hall modified to create a "little red schoolhouse" next to their dormitory. The Mexican and American flags lined the blackboard, which was adorned with the bilingual slogan "Mexico y los Estados Unidos son buenos amigos—Mexico and the United States are good friends." The Milwaukee Road also paid for baseball equipment for games at the North Thirty-Fifth Street and West Clybourn Street playgrounds.

Though living in somewhat isolated quarters in the Menominee Valley, the guest workers also interacted with the more established Mexican and Mexican American community on Milwaukee's near south side. Practicing Catholics could attend a Mass every weekend presided over by Father Alfredo Scotti from the city's Mexican Mission of Our Lady of Guadalupe. The devout met in a makeshift chapel in the workers' small recreation hall, with Mexican and American flags hanging on the wall. Some *braceros*, such as railroad worker and Veracruz native Ricardo García Cano, also found love in their adopted homes. The young Ricardo married Catherine Tovar, American born but of Mexican descent, whom he met during one night on the town. The bilingual Catherine, who helped her new husband learn English, became a regular visitor to the railroad colony along with other Milwaukee friends.

Demand for wartime labor continued up until the last year of the fighting overseas. In January 1945, the Wisconsin office of farm labor procurement warned of an impending labor shortage due to a change in selective service regulations, which lifted deferments of men eighteen to twenty-five years old working in essential agricultural work. Beyond calling for fifty thousand nonfarmer youths and adults to join the farm effort, the office called for an increased number of German prisoners of war (around six thousand) and another five thousand laborers from Mexico, Jamaica, and Barbados. The migrant workers worked alongside German prisoners of war throughout the harvest season.

Torivio Rivera
with friends in
Carrollville, 1920s.

Courtesy of the Navarro family

Mexican immigrants entering the United States in the 1920s first had to pass
through a border inspection and pay an alien head tax.

Courtesy of Ray Bacalzo

An Independence Day celebration hosted by Sociedad Mutualista Hispano-Azteca in Milwaukee in 1935.

Courtesy of Dennis Haro

The Haro family is pictured outside Our Lady of Guadalupe in Milwaukee in the 1930s.

Courtesy of the Rios Family

A group of children outside Our Lady of Guadalupe church in Milwaukee, after receiving their first communion.

Courtesy of the Navarro family

A family party for Bonifacio Navarro in Carollville in the late 1930s.

When members of Milwaukee's Mexican community enlisted in the US armed forces during World War II, some of their families placed these photographs at Our Lady of Guadalupe Mission Catholic Church. While many Mexican Americans were killed in the war, the men in the photographs all returned to their families afterward.

Left: The Sandoval family during a 1947 blizzard in Milwaukee.

Below: In 1948 Plymouth, a Mexican woman and her six children stand on the porch of the multifamily housing provided to them by the pea cannery that employed her husband.

Courtesy of Margarita Sandoval Skare

WHI IMAGE ID 22900

Right: José Cárdenas outside his grocery store in Milwaukee in the 1950s.

Below: Mexican American students take part in a celebration at South Division High School in Milwaukee in 1952.

Courtesy of Joseph Cárdenas

Courtesy of Ray Bacalzo

Left: Graciela and Luis De La Cruz, dancing in Milwaukee in the 1950s.

Below: José Martinez and his orquestra, known in Milwaukee as the "Mambo Kings," play at the Eagles Ballroom in 1955.

Courtesy of Graciela and Luis De La Cruz

Courtesy of Ray Bacalzo

This bunk bed was used by the family of Antonia and Aurelia Contreras, migrant agricultural workers from Mercedes, Texas. Three generations of the Contreras family worked on Waushara County cucumber farms from the 1940s through the 1980s.

WHS MUSEUM OBJECT ID 1999.16.1A-G

WHS MUSEUM OBJECT ID 1999.131.1

A scene painted by Seferina Contreras Klinger from memory shows her grandmother, Aurelia M. Contreras, and her uncle, Fidel Contreras, picking cucumbers on the Marks Brothers farm in Wautoma in the 1960s. Aurelia was in her eighties and Fidel in his sixties in the time period of the painting.

✖❧✖

LOS TEJANOS: TEXAS-MEXICAN MIGRANTS

Following the dramatic food drive of World War II, the number of Wisconsin crops raised and harvested for canning leaped upward in the subsequent decade. Before the start of the war, individual farmers would harvest their own crops and deliver them to canneries the following day. By the early 1950s, however, farmers were responsible for hundreds of thousands of acres of fields with peas, sweet corn, cucumbers for pickles, cherries, snap peas, lima beans, red and sugar beets, and tomatoes. While demand for laborers grew, the rural population of the state continued to fall percentagewise as thousands of workers moved away from farms to find work in urban areas. After the war, farmers shifted from commissioning foreign labor to recruiting domestic migrant workers, the majority of whom came from the American Southwest. In the immediate postwar years, nearly 85 percent of migrant workers employed by Wisconsin farmers were Texans of Mexican descent, also known as Tejanos (Texas Mexicans). Many Tejanos came from families that had lived in Texas since before the state joined the union in 1845 and as such were full US citizens.

The Tejanos had traveled to Wisconsin as migrant laborers for decades, mostly working in the sugar beet industry during the 1930s. The 1947 harvests signaled a sea change, however, as migrants spread across the entire state to new regions and different industries. Employers in need of laborers coordinated with the Wisconsin State Employment Service (WSES), a state agency established in 1948, to determine avenues of recruitment and develop migrant programs. Wisconsin employers would file requests with the WSES for the number of workers they required to fill out their harvest crews. After establishing that local laborers had been exhausted, the WSES would then work with a network of state employment services in Texas and other southern and southwest recruitment states such as Oklahoma, Arkansas, Louisiana, and Kentucky. The WSES first established an office in Door County in 1949 to assist with the cherry harvest, and then another office in Waushara County in 1950 for the cucumber harvest.

The number of Tejanos arriving in Wisconsin grew dramatically throughout the late 1940s and early 1950s. These migrants were reported in twenty-three of the state's seventy-one counties during the summer of

1947, totaling more than five thousand workers and their families. The largest concentrations were in rural towns including Wautoma, Rosendale, Oconto, Lomira, and Fox Lake. By the 1950s, ten to fourteen thousand migrant laborers, the vast majority of whom were Tejanos, made their way to Wisconsin every summer, helping the state keep its lead in the canning of peas, sweet corn, and beets. Those arriving in Wisconsin were part of an estimated yearly migration of one hundred thousand Texans swinging through the central states, including Ohio, Minnesota, Illinois, Iowa, Montana, and the Dakotas. The migrant crew usually consisted of a group of families, ranging from ten to thirty men, women and children, who traveled by car and covered truck.

Employers and receiving communities were not prepared for the sudden increase in Tejano migrants. While some families did have access to housing with running water, electricity, and adequate sanitation, many lived in rustic shacks, often shared with other families. According to reports, one-third of the housing units were unfit for human occupancy. An early survey of these communities found a direct relationship could be traced between a lack of contact between the employing farmer and the laboring family and the prevalence of substandard housing. Throughout the late 1940s, most migrant children did not attend Wisconsin schools during the fall harvest season; to help support their families, many children worked in the fields with their parents. Those children who did try to attend school could not expect to find bilingual teachers able to communicate with them in Spanish.

Besides unprepared migrant camps, Tejano workers also often faced prejudice and segregation in farming communities surrounding the fields in which they worked. Such discrimination was prevalent in Door County, where orchardists had turned to Tejano and African American migrant workers to compensate for fewer student workers and growing crop yields. The laborers and their families, brought to the northern counties to pick the bumper cherry crop, posed what the *Milwaukee Journal* referred to as the "Cherryland Problem." Crammed together in unsanitary shanties and living without proper medical attention, migrant workers also dealt with unfulfilled wage promises, often being paid at less than half the rate at which they had been contracted. Community businesses instituted a de facto segregation policy, as many eating establishments displayed "whites only" and "we cater only to whites" signs in their windows. White, African American, Mexican, American Indian, and

Jamaican laborers all lived in segregated quarters, while migrant camp directors offered the well-worn canard that the workers preferred to "be among people of their own kind." Resort owners were also bitter at the presence of the migrants, claiming that African American and Mexican workers drove away their customers, even though few if any ever ventured to the resort areas of the region. District attorney Edward G. Minor offered that the best solution might be to set stricter restrictions on the movement of migrants in the area, constraining them strictly to their work camps.

The Division for Children and Youth of the Wisconsin State Department of Public Welfare conducted a study of migrant workers in Door County in 1951. The study aimed to help the local community extend its services to migrant workers and coordinate planning, as well as give the department some exposure to the migrant community. Because of the unpredictable nature of crop harvesting over ten thousand acres of cherry orchards, employers did not offer contracts to workers but instead paid them at a piecework rate. When harvest yields were lower than expected, this practice would leave migrants stranded in the region without work or pay. The study also documented conflicts between migrants and tourists visiting the county's resorts, as growers did little to provide recreational activities for families, and travelers begrudged their presence in Door County's vacation spots. Social and religious organizations attempted to provide support for migrant workers in response to the study's findings. The Door County United Church Women engaged social workers to serve the migrant camps during the 1952 season, while a mayor's committee in Sturgeon Bay established a school for migrant children at one of the primary orchards, where students from four to eight years old were given instruction in math, English, and music.

Similar racial and cultural conflicts flared up between Tejano migrants and Wisconsinites across the state in the late 1940s. Struggles over recreational spaces in Waupun resulted in especially embarrassing media attention for town officials. During the summer of 1949, a Fond du Lac park custodian barred Tejano children and their families from swimming in the town pool because of their Mexican descent and their use of Spanish. When asked by the local press why he had restricted their entry, the custodian declared, "They say these people are American citizens. When you become an American citizen you should talk the language. Lots of these people don't." The park official further claimed that migrants might be carrying polio, and said that he would rather close the entire pool than let the Tejanos enter.

The Fond du Lac pool custodian's actions prompted swift backlash from community organizations and town officials. The League of Women Voters of Waupun, which had been working with area churches to provide recreational activities for the Tejano families, appealed the park officer's restriction of migrants to town officials. League representatives argued that the children were American citizens and were therefore entitled to the same privileges as other Wisconsinites. County officials worried about the negative messages the "racial difficulties" in their community might send to the migrants' home communities in Texas, and how they might affect the future ability of local farmers to recruit Tejanos for work. Within a matter of days, the Fond du Lac county parks committee, under advisement from the county attorney, issued a statement "refusing to tolerate any discrimination" in county parks. The committee forced the offending custodian to resign.

In response to the discrimination against Tejano children and under pressure from organizations such as the League of Women Voters, civic and religious leaders formed a community council on human relations. The committee hoped to break down social prejudices by working across racial lines and increasing contact between the two communities. Coordinating with the Wisconsin Governor's Commission on Human Rights, the ad hoc group created a summer education and recreation program for the more than two hundred migratory laborers working in the potato, onion, and sugar beet crops the following summer. The school boards of Dodge and Fond du Lac Counties provided textbooks and use of building space for classes in English for children and their parents, while park officials offered supplies for ball games and picnics. Despite the success of the educational and recreational activities, however, the program did nothing to alleviate the poor housing, sanitation, and working conditions the migrants faced.

In light of ongoing discrimination against Tejanos, state officials and media hoping to protect the state's economic future implored Wisconsinites to welcome the migrants. Rebecca C. Barton, director of the Governor's Commission on Human Rights, asked the state's citizens to welcome the arriving migrants because of their economic importance: "From the migrant point of view, home is wherever they find it in the hearts of friendly people. From the community point of view, it is good business to treat the migrant decently because he is an economic asset." The editorial board of the *Milwaukee Sentinel* agreed that migrants deserved "a friendly hand and a fair shake." As migrants made the difference between success and failure in many of the state's harvesting operations, the workers deserved "decent treatment while they are giving it." The editorial board hoped that communities around the state would follow Waupun's lead by implementing school projects for migrant children and advocating for decent housing, recreational programs, and health measures for Tejanos.

Reported discrimination and inhumane living and working conditions also provoked statewide investigations into the "migrant situation." The Wisconsin Governor's Commission on Human Rights produced the study "Migratory Agricultural Workers in Wisconsin: A Problem in Human Rights" in 1950. Composed of government officials, community members, clergy, and university professors, the commission responsible for the report investigated the employment, health, housing, and education of migrants and documented instances of discrimination and prejudice in receiving communities. President Harry Truman convened a similar national committee in 1950 called the Presidential Commission on Migrant Labor, on which Professor Noble Clark, associate director of the Agricultural Experiment Station at the University of Wisconsin, served as well. Both the Wisconsin and national reports noted numerous abuses that included low wages, intimidation of workers, malnutrition, and inadequate education for migrant adults and children.

The authors of the Wisconsin report referenced John Steinbeck's *The Grapes of Wrath* and Carey McWilliams's *Factories in the Fields* as recognizable reference points for readers to describe the plight of migrant workers in Wisconsin. Like the workers described in these classic texts, Tejano migrants arriving in Wisconsin faced the possibility of having been sold a false bill of goods if employers fraudulently misrepresented employment opportunities in the state. Often, agricultural employers, not knowing the yield for the year's harvest, would over-recruit workers, a situation that left unemployed migrant families in desperate need of pay and shelter. Over-recruitment also served as an established tactic to suppress wage rates, as employers could more readily pull from an enlarged pool of available (and for employers, dispensable) labor. In order to find continuous employment throughout the summer's shifting crop seasons, migrant families often had to move three or four times during their Wisconsin stays. A family might begin the summer planting sugar beets, move along to interim employment in the cherry or pickle industry, and then move back to finish the season harvesting beets.

The surplus of labor also meant that employers could get away with providing less in the way of adequate living spaces. Many migrants lived in either the crude barracks that had been used by foreign migrants or prisoners of war during World War II, which had been built for single men and had not been inspected in years, or in abandoned farm buildings in various states of disrepair. The appalling conditions described in the Governor's Commission's reports helped lead to the creation of permanent governmental committees and the passage of new laws designed to protect migrant workers in Wisconsin. In 1953, the Governor's Commission created the State Migrant Committee under the auspices of the Wisconsin Welfare Council, with representatives from state departments, churches, and other concerned groups. As most federal and state law excluded agricultural labor from wage and hour protections, even for the Tejanos who were US citizens, Wisconsin legislators needed to craft legislation in a piecemeal fashion to address migrant issues. Under pressure from advocates calling for better enforcement of registration, inspection, and certification of migrant camps, the state legislature began reform by passing laws affecting migrants' housing, minimum wages, child labor protections, and social insurance and public assistance in 1951. Standing in strong opposition to the new state initiatives were employers and employer organizations such as the Wisconsin Canners and Freezers Association, which decried such laws as governmental meddling throughout the decade.

Federal and state officials returned to migrant issues periodically throughout the 1950s. In October 1959, a United States Senate Subcommittee on Migratory Labor convened in Madison to discuss ways to better the living and working conditions of the more than eleven thousand migrant workers in Wisconsin. More than twenty witnesses presented on migrants' low incomes; inadequate housing, sanitation, and medical care; and sparse educational opportunities for Spanish-speaking children. In his remarks, Governor Gaylord Nelson expressed his support for providing employment with a guaranteed minimum wage, schooling with support from state and federal aid, a more robust state and federal welfare system, and better health care for workers. Elected officials and representatives from a growers' association also debated the minimum age for agricultural employment, with congressmen favoring fourteen years of age as a minimum rather than twelve years as preferred by growers. In response to the criticisms of worker treatment, the president of the Wisconsin Farm Bureau Federation opposed all reforms presented to the committee as unnecessary federal and state interference in private agricultural industry.

While government action to address these issues came slowly, religious organizations answered the call across Wisconsin to increase outreach to Tejanos through migrant ministry programs. Catholic clerical leaders rushed to train seminarians in Spanish, while laity provided early schooling for children, health services, and education for workers on their civil rights as American citizens. In Green Bay, Bishop Stanislaus V. Bona initiated an innovative migrant ministry program in 1948 that administered to the spiritual and physical needs of Tejanos throughout cherry and cucumber fields in northeastern Wisconsin.

Through church-run programs, more than two thousand migrants gained access to religious education, child care, adult education, organized sports, and leadership training classes in 1951 alone. Clergy and laity publicized the plight of migrant workers, who were often left jobless and hungry in down periods, were shut out of local schools and churches, and were ignored or resented by the communities in which they worked. In January 1958, Reverend Ogle Chastain, chairman of evangelism and state missions of the Wisconsin Baptist State Convention, implored church leaders, employers, and public officials to work together to provide for the state's thirteen thousand migrant workers. Chastain, quoted in the *Milwaukee Sentinel* in 1958, called specifically for Protestants to have a unified voice on advocating for legislation for migrant laborers: "We ask them to come to Wisconsin to harvest the crops because the canning industry needs them. Their presence affords us an opportunity for brotherhood which we should not pass up."

Tejano migrant workers scattered throughout the state of Wisconsin, sometimes in areas where communities had never seen or heard Spanish before. In Hawkins, a small village in Rusk County, Arturo Landeros and his family were the only Spanish speakers in the county, and perhaps the only permanent residents of Mexican descent in northwestern Wisconsin in 1958. Both Landeros and his wife were native-born US citizens, originally from Laredo, Texas. After serving in the Marine Corps during World War II, Landeros had managed crews of migrant laborers working in bean and potato fields during summer seasons for many years. Deciding to retire from the migrant life, the Landeros family had originally looked at farms to purchase in the Oconto area, where they had worked for many summers in the potato fields. Instead, they settled in Rusk County in 1957 on a 160-acre farm, where they got their first taste of the rugged northern Wisconsin winters. The transplanted Tejanos got along very well with their Ukrainian neighbors, who were themselves displaced after World War II.

Elsewhere, Tejano families arriving in large numbers transformed communities. By the late 1950s, the *Milwaukee Sentinel* reported that Mexican-descent migrant workers had "taken over" the "onetime Scandinavian citadel" of Wautoma, where Norwegians became the minority during the summer months. Tejano migrants, who numbered more than 4,300 in Waushara County, could also be found working in the adjoining communities of Berlin, Red Granite, Wild Rose, Plainfield, Hancock, and other towns in the "pickle belt," where cucumber ruled. Bars and shops displayed the red, white, and green flags of Mexico while Spanish-language films played in movie theatres. The Salas' Café served Mexican dishes such as enchiladas, tacos, tamales, and menudo de res, and grocery stores carried lutefisk next to hot peppers and bottled tamale sauce. In Marquette County, Spanish had become the "new language" heard throughout local banks and restaurants thanks to the more than one thousand people of Mexican descent living in the region seasonally. In an effort to engender better relations between farmers and the new workers, the townspeople and farmers of Baxter attended Spanish classes, learning words and expressions that they might need for daily interactions with the migrants. The citizens of Montello also initiated a special advisory program that visited migrant camps and proposed initiatives to improve housing and educational opportunities.

✣

IMMIGRATION AND DOCUMENTATION

While Tejano migrants became the largest newly arriving Spanish-speaking population throughout the 1950s, Mexican nationals continued to make their way to Wisconsin throughout the decade. A small number of Mexicans came as guest workers through renewed labor agreements between the United States and Mexico, but others found their way to the state through extralegal means. The *Milwaukee Journal* referred to undocumented Mexicans working in the state as "wetbacks" in a June 1950 article, a derogatory term used during the period to refer to the immigrants' unlawful presence in the country.

Enforcement of immigration law and deportation proceedings was at times uneven and dependent on an employer's desire to maintain a consistent workforce. According to A. B. Clegg, chief of the Milwaukee Office of Immigration and Naturalization, about fifteen Mexican aliens were deported from the Milwaukee area each month during the summer in the early 1950s, a number that would have been higher had the office had more immigration agents and resources. Clegg estimated that hundreds of undocumented immigrants made their way to Wisconsin in the summer months. He viewed their arrival somewhat ambivalently as they were valuable workers for farmers and canneries. While some Mexicans made their way to the state on their own, many employers also recruited heavily through company agents in Texas to bring workers north. Ignoring federal regulations to expand their labor pools quickly, these company agents did not verify the workers' immigration status upon recruitment. Even when arrested, undocumented workers were usually given probation and allowed to return to their jobs in the fields for the remainder of the summer, because immigration officials recognized their economic importance to the state.

But anti-immigrant sentiment and support for deportation were growing among the populace at large throughout the 1950s. State newspapers spoke out against the undocumented Mexicans in the state, often reverting to racist stereotypes and fearmongering to justify their call for renewed deportations. The *Milwaukee Journal* editorial board argued in numerous editorials for the continuation of President Dwight D. Eisenhower's deportation program known as "Operation Wetback," which by 1953 had detained hundreds of thousands of Mexican workers attempting to enter the country without documentation. Calling the situation an "invasion," the editors warned that for every "wetback" caught, another successfully crossed the border. Parroting claims made by the paper's editors a few decades earlier, the *Milwaukee Journal* claimed, without reference to facts or study, that undocumented immigrants were more likely to have mental, physical, and moral defects, to be drains on public assistance programs, and to be engaged in marijuana or heroin drug trafficking.

Mexican immigrants found that local immigration officials enforced immigration laws arbitrarily, with little rhyme or reason from case to case. Mexican nationals living in this country were not afforded, for example, the same protections and exemptions within immigration law as European immigrants received throughout the 1950s for safe passage and stay. Under the McCarran-Wolter Immigration Act, undocumented Mexicans fearing deportation could not access the "hardship" exemptions available to European immigrants. Milwaukee resident Gregorio Salazar, who came to the United States by crossing the border without proper documentation at the age of seventeen in 1942, faced these legal discrepancies firsthand in 1953. Upon settling in Wisconsin, Salazar married Adeline Romaine, an Appleton resident of German and French descent, and they had four children. After a review of immigration records in 1953, immigration officials notified Salazar that he would be deported. The family's four children, all American citizens, were removed from the home and placed under the care of the county home for dependent children. Salazar had no criminal record, had learned English, had made a home for himself and his family in Milwaukee, and at the time worked as the top salesperson for a wholesale food producer. Upon hearing of his impending deportation, the CEO and president of his employer attempted to intervene through the office of their congressmen, to no end. Members of the Mexican community also organized through the Mexican Catholic parish of Our Lady of Guadalupe, with aid from lawyers and representatives from charity organizations helping brainstorm ideas to stay the deportation order.

To avoid long-term expulsion from the United States, Salazar voluntarily returned to Mexico under an agreement reached with immigration officials. After living in Mexico for an enforced period of two months, Salazar successfully petitioned for a visa and passport to return to Milwaukee in September 1953, being able to do so only because of his marriage to an American citizen. Upon arriving at the family home on National Avenue, Salazar found the house empty. He soon learned from a neighbor that his wife was at the county hospital, where she had just given birth to their fifth child. Despite having made these irregular agreements with immigration officials and following their final ruling, Salazar was forced to wait three years before applying for US citizenship. Ultimately, experiences such as Salazar's meant that many Mexican immigrants living throughout Wisconsin carried fear and apprehension with them daily. Moreover, federal enforcement campaigns such as Operation Wetback and the ensuing newspaper coverage of deportation raids subjected all Mexicans to the unjust blanket stigma of being unlawfully present in their new communities—regardless of their actual documentation status.

⚜

MIGRANT MINISTRY

Protestant and Catholic laypeople, clergy, and seminarians continued their mission of serving the spiritual and educational needs of the state's migrant workers throughout the 1960s. In the first summer of the decade, more than fifty staff members from various denominations worked throughout the state's migrant camps. They provided worship services and Masses, educational programs, health advisement, and recreational activities for families, which were conducted by clergymen with transportation provided for migrants.

The Milwaukee Catholic Archdiocese, having sponsored the migrant ministry program over the previous ten years, institutionalized their efforts in 1960 with the appointment of Reverend George Kolanda of Cudahy as a permanent outreach coordinator to migrant workers. Other religious orders also stepped up their support throughout the 1960s. Working with clergy and lay volunteers, the School Sisters of St. Francis organized religious schools in Beaver Dam, Wautoma, Belgium, and Random Lake that served hundreds of children brought by bus. Along with facilitating educational services, the sisters also distributed clothes, blankets, and religious materials to families, while nurses administered polio shots.

The Wisconsin Council of Churches expanded Protestant outreach to migrants as well, joining a nationwide effort initiated by the National Council of Churches (NCC) that had begun forty years earlier and spread over thirty-three states. The Protestants' approach stressed empathy and understanding for the plight of the workers they served. NCC's former president Reverend Eugene Carson Blake told the *Milwaukee Sentinel* in 1961 that he believed "one day of picking berries in the field would be the best training for any Christian who wants to help migrants." Over the course of the decade, the NCC provided religious services that traveled across farms—called "churches on wheels"—for 250,000 migrant farmworkers per year in thirty states, including Wisconsin. In January 1963, the Wisconsin Council of Churches approved a stepped-up program for ministry to migrant workers in the fields with more funding for health education, food and clothing, and religious services. The new funds also covered periodic surveys, analyses of migration trends, and frequent conferences to review results.

In migrant farmworker camps where Mexican and Tejano workers settled for the growing and harvesting seasons, hastily constructed chapels at times functioned as the center for community and education. In the central Wisconsin village of Endeavor, La Casa de Nuestra Señora de Guadalupe (the House of Our Lady of Guadalupe) offered classes for youth, free medical and dental care, and a social scene for those of all ages. Founded in 1958, La Casa served a core of one thousand migrants representing 135 families by the end of the 1960s. Volunteers erected La Casa's chapel in 1960, the first permanent structure in the area the migrants could call their own. Made of knotty boards forming a country-cathedral ceiling and pink, green, yellow, and blue tinted glass forming the outside wall, the chapel also featured a mosaic of broken glass bottles that had been placed by hand by migrant children. Each Sunday after Mass, volunteers operated a rummage sale where clothes and furniture were sold at a discount. The center also funded religious and academic schools. Physicians from Marquette and Columbia Counties and from St. Mary's Hospital in Madison staffed the church-run clinic, open three days a week. In the medical center alone, volunteers served at least ten newborns and their mothers every week, with more than fifty patients passing through medical screenings weekly. Because of the especially erratic nature of migrant life, however, permanent chapels like the one at Endeavor were difficult to plan for and maintain across growing multiple seasons.

Some clergy and volunteers around the state committed to becoming bilingual and learning about Mexican culture to better serve their new parishioners. In the small town of Princeton in central Wisconsin, the rapid influx of Tejano migrants prompted Reverend Josef Cieciorka, pastor of St. John the Baptist, to engage in a crash course program of self-instruction by way of books and audio recordings to learn Spanish as quickly as possible. Cieciorka used his rudimentary language skills to create bilingual signs to post throughout migrant camps in the area inviting Spanish-speaking workers to Mass.

In anticipation of joining the Catholic Migrant Apostolate of Green Bay, seminary students from Clintonville and Green Bay traveled to San Antonio, Texas, in 1962 to live among migrants who would travel to Wisconsin for the harvest season. The seminarians hitchhiked as far south as Mexico City to learn Spanish and as much about Mexican culture as they could before returning to their studies. Bishops and program coordinators also recognized the need to engage their pastors in language and cultural education throughout the decade. In 1962, the Milwaukee Catholic Archdiocese initiated a pilot program at Marquette University to train priests for assignment among twenty-five thousand Spanish-speaking residents in the region. Migrant workers lacked comparable access to instruction, but many learned to speak English over time through contact with their employers and communities. Outreach from bilingual volunteers helped facilitate this process and minimize their cultural isolation throughout the mid-twentieth century.

≫❧≪

A GROWING FOCUS ON THE
MIGRANT WORKERS' PLIGHT

Prompted by public criticism from clerical leaders, state politicians moved to enforce some semblance of reform for migrant laborers in the Wisconsin agricultural industry. The work of the Governor's Commission a decade earlier had yielded little in the way of actual progress, so Governor Gaylord Nelson appointed a new special Committee on Migratory Labor to identify major concerns within the migrant community and to help coordinate the activities of state and voluntary agencies working to face labor and social problems among laborers in 1960. Led by University of Wisconsin–Madison professor Elizabeth Brandeis Raushenbush, who went on to become a leader in the movement supporting labor protections for migrants, the committee toured migrant camps across the state to provide a full picture of their situation. The commission's scathing final report documented what members believed to be the "evils inherent in migratory work." The study outlined many of the issues missionaries and social service organizations had identified since the late 1940s: substandard housing, subpar wages, inadequate medical and health standards, and nearly nonexistent educational opportunities for the children of migrant workers. The commission reported that migrants traveled thousands of miles in crowded and unreliable cars, trucks, or buses to get to Wisconsin in hopes of finding better-paying positions to provide for their families, only to discover living and working conditions well below the standard the state had established for its own residents and industrial laborers. Outside the fields in which they worked, Tejanos were also regarded as foreigners. Regardless of their citizenship status, their dark skin and accented English made them targets of discrimination in local towns.

In light of the migrant workforce's economic necessity for the state's agricultural market, the commission's findings presented a number of problems for Wisconsin legislators and employment recruiters. State employment coordinators at the Wisconsin State Employment Service (WSES) deemed Tejanos indispensable for the annual cucumber seasons in Portage and Waushara Counties. In fact, one of the state's most important agricultural harvests would be impossible without their labor, and without better treatment the state risked losing its labor supply. Recognizing this, agencies initiated several state-funded programs to mitigate health and education needs within the migrant community. The annual influx of migrant children during harvest seasons presented a number of linguistic and technical challenges for educators. These children lacked regular access to classrooms because of their migratory lifestyle, and they lagged as many as five years below grade level. The Governor's Committee on Migratory Labor debated the best methods to provide education for migrant children throughout the 1960s, proposing summer school programming, day care centers, outreach through the University of Wisconsin Cooperative Extension Services, and renewed aid for local education efforts. Catholic and Protestant religious groups helped fill the gaps by founding schools for migrant workers in areas around the state, including Belgium, Random Lake, Sturgeon Bay, and

Green Bay. While not able to reach all migrant children living in Wisconsin due to limited resources, these schools attempted to cater to the needs of students with bilingual teachers and transportation, as well as religious services and medical aid, including vaccinations.

The state started its first Spanish-language Head Start Program in 1962 in Wautoma, where bilingual student teachers from Alverno College provided early education to young migrant students throughout the early 1960s. Also in 1962, Wisconsin established its first state-sponsored day-care center for migrant children, carried out under the Division of Children and Youth in the state Department of Public Welfare. The first year of the program's operation included six weeks of day care for thirty-five youngsters, aged three to seven years old, at the Spring Lake schoolhouse, staffed by professional educators, psychologists, and bilingual trained aides. Program coordinators advertised the day care through bilingual posters displayed in camps. Despite receiving only a small amount of starter funds to begin the program, the day-care center received immediate criticism from some growers, who felt that their migrant workers were receiving too much aid from the state.

The termination of the national Bracero program in 1964 prompted even larger statewide concern regarding the treatment of Tejano migrant workers. In Wisconsin, growers had moved away from the recruitment of *braceros* following the end of World War II, instead shifting toward domestic migrant Tejano labor. In 1962, only 638 Mexican nationals made their way to the state to labor in agricultural work. Across the country, employers had also shifted away from the guest worker program and toward domestic labor as the costs associated with the transportation and housing of braceros became more and more expensive. The use of machinery on farms also contributed to the labor shift. In Wisconsin, growers employed 23 pea-harvesting combines in 1958, but by 1963 that number had grown to 325. Beyond labor considerations, the program had faced attacks from migrant advocates, church groups, and labor unions as inhumane and exploitative. Critics asked why different standards existed for migrant agricultural and industrial workers. As migrant minister Reverend John Maurice of Waukesha told the *Milwaukee Journal* in 1963:

> The question everyone ignores when talking about the bracero program is the human one. Put it in terms of Milwaukee: Who

would allow a manufacturer, who pays slave wages and has improper working conditions, to operate here? No one would want to work for him. Would we allow that company to import people from Japan or Africa because he refuses to meet just demands? I think not. Therefore why allow large corporate growers to do it?

Organizations such as the AFL-CIO argued that *braceros* depressed wages and working conditions for domestic migrant workers, and that the program allowed for the trafficking of human beings as mere commodities to be abused at the whim of employers. Wisconsin's own Senator William Proxmire rose as one of the program's most vocal critics, who argued against the continuation of a "slave measure" that held both Mexican national and migrant workers in subhuman working and living conditions.

The program's discontinuation raised alarm among the state's farmers and canners, who feared the indirect consequences of the agreement's end on Wisconsin's labor force. Although the state's share of bracero workers was marginal in comparison to states such as California and Texas, who recruited more than two hundred thousand workers per year, the end of the program increased the nationwide demand for domestic migrant workers. Wisconsin employers feared that increased workforce competition with southwestern and southern farmers would lead to rising labor costs in the state. WSES officials warned that Wisconsin growers would be at a disadvantage in recruiting Tejano workers, as the cherry and cucumber harvests lasted only from six to eight weeks, while California growers could offer longer periods of stable employment for crops harvested in their state. Migrant Tejanos knew from travelling the seasonal labor circuit, however, that working and living conditions throughout the Midwest, Southwest, and Northwest would often be substandard and inhumane, regardless of the region or employer.

ORGANIZING IN THE FIELDS: OBREROS UNIDOS

As demand for Tejano labor increased, migrant farmworkers across the country found themselves in a stronger position to fight for better treatment. Frustrated by the slow movement to improve their deplorable working conditions and inspired by the budding labor movement of farmworkers in California, Tejano migrants in Wisconsin began to organize for their rights as workers. Like migrant laborers around the country, those in Wisconsin had faced a number of difficulties in fighting for improved working and living conditions. The very nature of transient migrant labor made it easier for growers to disrupt organizing among workers, as they could simply choose to not rehire a worker perceived to be an agitator the following growing season. Organizing scattered groups of laborers in constant motion presented a particular challenge for migrant labor leaders.

Perhaps no person was more instrumental in organizing migrant farmworkers throughout the 1960s than Jesus Salas, a third-generation Texas-born Mexican American farmworker in Wautoma. Salas's parents had been migrant farmworkers traveling throughout the United States since the 1940s. In 1958, the couple bought a restaurant in Wautoma and settled in Wisconsin permanently to give their children more stable educational opportunities. From 1961 to 1965, Jesus Salas worked during the summers in day-care programs for migrant children provided through local churches and the Wisconsin State Division of Child and Youth. In 1965, Salas, then a junior at Stevens Point State University, was hired by University of Wisconsin professor Elizabeth Brandies Raushenbush to conduct a study of migrants in the Wautoma area. Working with his brother Manuel, Salas learned more about the workers' piecemeal wages and substandard living conditions, as well as about state labor and migrant employment laws. Spurred on by his findings and his own family history, Salas joined the Midwestern branch of the National Farm Workers Association (NFWA), a new organization under the leadership of community activist and soon-to-be labor leader César Chávez that was working to unionize agricultural workers in California and Texas.

Back in Wautoma, Salas joined with a multiethnic coalition of organizers that included Tejanos Salvador Sanchez and Manuel Salas and university students Mark Erenburg and Bill Smith. Together, they began the process of uniting Wisconsin migrant workers in the cucumber-growing industry in the central region of the state into a labor union during the late summer of 1966. The organizational drive represented the first sustained effort to form a migrant farmworker labor union in the Great Lakes Region. Focused on reaffirming the dignity of migrant farmworkers throughout the state of Wisconsin, the workers demanded improved wages, better living and working conditions, and input on the day-to-day decisions that affected their lives. The migrant workers chose Obreros Unidos, or Workers United, as the name of their new organization and adopted the slogan "La Raza Se Junta" ("Our People Rise to the Cause") as their rallying cry.

Tejano migrants lived and worked in Wisconsin for only a few months a year, making it difficult to reach out to such a large number of workers and have them commit to a union. To offset this challenge, migrant activists began their organizing in Texas, speaking to workers before they began their annual voyage to Wisconsin. The organizers found an advantage in organizing among politically mobilized migrants hailing from southwestern Texas. Many of the migrants who made their way to the Midwest annually hailed from borderland towns such as Crystal City, where a politically active Mexican American community had successfully secured electoral victories in the city council in the early 1960s.

Under the leadership of twenty-two-year-old Jesus Salas, migrants in Wautoma organized a march to Madison in August 1966 to raise awareness of the deprived conditions under which laborers worked and lived. Twenty-four marchers representing more than five thousand migrant laborers employed in Waushara, Portage, and Marquette Counties pledged to walk the eighty miles separating their camps from the state's capitol in a protest the workers referred to as a "march for respectability" for Tejano migrants. The march's organizers carried with them four key demands: a raise in the minimum wage for agricultural workers, as Wisconsin's farmworker wages amounted to only a fraction of the nonagricultural wages in the period; coverage under the state's workmen's compensation law and health insurance; migrant labor representation on the Governor's Committee on Migratory Labor; and public sanitation facilities for migrant workers in Wautoma.

Hoping to avoid negative press and stop the march, more than twenty representatives from the Wisconsin State Industrial Commission promised the migrants to act on their demands in due time. State Industrial Commission chairman Joseph C. Fagan deemed the call for minimum wage guarantees and better living conditions to be reasonable and fair and promised to find a sensible solution to the migrants' qualms. Fagan's assurances were not enough to discourage the marchers, however.

With state officials' efforts unable to prevent the protest, Salas rallied more than two hundred supporters on the steps of the Wautoma courthouse the Sunday before the march. Representatives from the NFWA's Midwest office attended the rally, bringing with them the encouragement of Chávez. In a telegram to Salas and the migrants, Chávez encouraged the young marchers by stating, "The time is past due for all Americans to recognize the right of farmworkers to dignity, equality and the same legislative protection which is extended to all other workers in the United States." Chávez also sent a telegram to Wisconsin governor Warren Knowles urging him to "extend full support and cooperation to the march." Following the rally, the assembled protesters met for a special Mass and benediction at St. Joseph's Catholic Church under Father Michael Garrigan, who then pledged to join the workers along with other religious leaders such as Reverend Barry Shaw, director of the Wisconsin Council of Churches.

The following Monday, the migrant workers began their five-day march. On the first day they made stops through Coloma and then marched south along State Highway 51. The protesters carried banners with the Virgin of Guadalupe and signs in Spanish bearing the thunderbird made famous by Chávez's United Farm Workers union in California, as well as an American flag. Migrants camped overnight or stayed at supportive Methodist and Lutheran churches along the way. By the time the group reached the steps of the state capitol later that week, the march had grown to more than 150 people, including migrant workers from around the state, priests, nuns, ministers, and students. Along the way, supporters greeted the marchers with donations collected for their cause. Addressing the assembled crowd at the steps of the capitol, an appreciative Salas said: "We marched 80 miles to show a social and economic problem exists. The state of Wisconsin has a progressive tradition and must alleviate these problems." The migrant workers then moved into the governor's conference room to meet with representatives from the state industrial commission to discuss the marchers' demands.

While not successful in securing assurances for all of their demands, the migrants' march did begin a statewide conversation regarding the living and working conditions of Tejano workers. In the years immediately following the march, two migrant representatives secured positions on the Governor's Committee on Migrant Labor, while state officials pushed for the construction of public sanitary facilities in central Wisconsin camps. In addition, the Governor's Committee commissioned a study of migrant wages in the cucumber industry and minimum wage laws affecting agricultural workers. It also directed state resources to provide stronger enforcement of housing codes for migrant dwellings.

The march was perhaps most effective in publicizing the plight of migrant workers across Wisconsin, spurring organizations to voice their support for worker organization. In November 1966, the Wisconsin Catholic Bishops' Commission for Spanish Speaking endorsed efforts by migrant workers to organize and bargain collectively. The commission, representing the five Catholic Wisconsin archdioceses, said in its statement, "Farm labor now stands in the pitiful posture of the exploited factory workers of the 19th century. . . . The union ideal which has elevated the trades to such heights and prospered the whole economy must now be extended to farm labor." In January 1967, delegates to the Wisconsin Council of Churches' annual convention likewise passed a resolution supporting collective bargaining rights for migrant farmworkers, and urged their respective churches to organize boycotts against growers who opposed open and fair labor negotiations.

Not surprisingly, Wisconsin growers disagreed vehemently with Obreros Unidos's contentions and grew upset that Salas had given the Wautoma area a black eye with the protests. Along with publicly pushing back against calls for an increased minimum wage, employers denied claims that they didn't provide safe and sanitary living and working conditions in their camps, going as far as inviting journalists to tour their facilities to verify their high standards. Faced with the costs of meeting their workers' demands and increased scrutiny from regulators, some turned to increased mechanization or even threatened to stop growing within Wisconsin. Companies such as Libby, McNeill & Libby increased funding toward research in emerging harvesting technologies. The Wisconsin Canners Association, meeting in Madison in 1961, first raised the possibility of replacing as many workers as possible with machines. Association leaders explained to plant representatives that they hoped machinery would make migrant workers a "rare" sight in Wisconsin within five years.

While growers' concerns about rising costs may have been genuine, their reactions also reflected racism that was common toward workers of Mexican descent. They called into question their employees' work habits, worrying that higher wages would simply encourage migrant laborers to work less for more. Robert Schramek, executive vice president of the Chicago Pickle Company, based out of Redgranite in Waushara County, explained to the *Milwaukee Journal*, "We'd be getting a lot of them up here who would just want to take it nice and easy and earn their $1.25 an hour. You'd also have to supervise them to make sure they worked." Schramek, parroting the beliefs of other Wisconsin growers, already suspected the migrants of having lazy work habits. He went as far as to imply that "some [workers] just come up here to get out of the hot Texas sun." Comments like these did much to inspire Obreros Unidos to continue fighting for dignity and respect on the job.

With energy running high after the migrant march and growers consolidating around tactics to stall labor organizing, Obreros Unidos embarked on an organizing and strike drive in October 1966 at a potato processing plant in Almond in the first attempt by migrant laborers to strike in Wisconsin history. After employers denied the demands of one hundred migrant workers for union recognition, the new union voted to engage in a nine-day strike. The striking workers received support from the Wisconsin AFL-CIO, which passed a resolution at its state convention and donated $2,500 to the cause. Although the walkout failed to win a contract for the workers, it did draw the attention of the state's vast vegetable growing and processing industries as well as organized labor, progressive groups, and church organizations. The strike also forced the state employment relations board to intervene, giving some hope that a future strike might be more successful. Through state arbitration, the union won some stipulations, including paid back wages, while state officials moved to sanction the plant owners for unfair labor practices.

Taking lessons from the Almond walkout, Obreros Unidos next targeted Libby, McNeil & Libby Company. The cucumber processor had actively resisted efforts to alleviate poor conditions in the previous decade. In the winter before the cucumber harvest of 1967, Salas traveled to Texas to meet with migrant workers who planned to travel to Wisconsin later that year. He spoke in people's homes, in union meetings and labor councils, and at civic events, doing his best to persuade Tejano migrants of the necessity of collective action through organized labor. Back in Wisconsin, organizers held meetings, published a monthly bilingual newspaper called *La Voz Mexicana*, and planned volunteer legal aid for migrants. In August 1967, with the support of a wide majority of workers, Obreros demanded to be recognized as the collective bargaining representative by Libby management and filed thirty complaints alleging violations of the minimum wage law by pickle processors in Waushara, Adams, and Portage Counties with the state.

Libby management refused to recognize the labor union or their leaders' call for a representation vote. With no compromise in sight, four hundred Obreros Unidos members representing 80 percent of the Libby workforce walked off the job on a half-day strike on August 23, and promised a full work stoppage of migrant workers if their employer failed to meet them at the bargaining table. After meeting with Salas and Libby management, the Wisconsin Employment Relations Commission (WERC) called for a prompt union recognition election. As the cucumber harvest was rapidly drawing to a close and migrant workers were set to leave the state for their next harvest season, WERC scheduled an expedient election before the end of the month. By a resounding majority, more than four hundred migrant workers at Libby voted to accept Obreros Unidos as their bargaining representative. WERC immediately certified Obreros as the exclusive labor union for the company's fieldworkers.

When initial bargaining meetings failed, though, Libby management decided to replace their migrant workforce with a mechanized harvesting system. The union filed an unfair labor practice complaint, but the state upheld the company's decision. Although Libby management was forced to bargain with Obreros over the mechanization process, as well as offer preferential hiring to former migrant workers for mechanized positions, the outcome struck a major blow to the union's collective bargaining position.

Despite the setback, Obreros Unidos's leadership continued to push state politicians to take a stand in fighting for migrant workers' rights. Attorney General Bronson La Follette, running for governor, toured four Wautoma migrant camps with Jesus Salas and other Obreros representatives in August 1968. Speaking in Spanish, the candidate explained to the laborers and their families that the state needed to do more for "the forgotten Americans—the migrant worker" and promised "to call attention to the plight of Wisconsin's migrants."

Wisconsin's farmworker campaign was also connected to national campaigns during the 1960s and early 1970s in a number of ways, perhaps most publicly through the national grape boycott. In the midst of a vigorous organizing drive in the grape industry in 1968, Chávez's United Farm Workers called for a national boycott of grapes and grape-related alcoholic products such as wine and brandy. Their hope was to force California growers to recognize migrants' right to unionize. In Wisconsin, Jesus Salas organized boycott actions across the state, focusing on buyers and grocery stores as well as providing picketing support against those stores that refused to respect the protests. The boycott drew supporters from across Wisconsin, ranging from middle-class suburbanites to labor leaders to students.

MEETING THE NEEDS OF DISPLACED WORKERS

As migrant laborers were still fighting for better working conditions, their jobs were rapidly disappearing, replaced by mechanization. State employment agents predicted that by 1972, 98 percent of the present migrant jobs would be eliminated in the state, with the majority of remaining positions located in the much harder to automate section of canning. For those migrant workers who were able to find employment in the state's fields, work could often be sporadic. Still angry from the contentious labor fights of the late 1960s, growers blamed organizations such as Obreros Unidos for speeding up the mechanization that led to work instability. Fewer migrant workers arrived in Wisconsin, and those who remained sought employment in urban areas. The permanent move from farms to cities and towns such as Milwaukee, Waukesha, and Appleton could often be jarring for migrants; language difficulties, a gap in job skills for industrial labor in factories and foundries, and cultural differences all served as barriers to full integration into these new communities.

As in previous decades, religious organizations led the efforts to meet the new set of needs of these urban workers. After decades of ministering to migrant workers through various education- and health-based programs, Catholic and Protestant organizations joined together in May 1965 to coordinate their efforts through an organization called United Migrant Opportunity Services, Incorporated (UMOS). Based out of Waukesha but serving migrants across the state, UMOS's coalitional efforts helped fill employment, educational, and social needs of workers constantly on the move across towns, counties, and states. UMOS first used federal grant money to open four day-care centers in Sturtevant, Portage, Hartford, and Muskego.

With a productive first year of programming under its belt, UMOS successfully petitioned for a larger grant of $979,000 in 1966 to assist twelve thousand farmworkers in thirteen Wisconsin counties. The majority of the new funds were allocated for adult education programs, along with day care and educational enrichment classes for migrant children. UMOS's growing efficacy in the fields led to an additional $1.2 million in federal funding in 1967, which allowed staff to expand day-care support to seventeen Wisconsin counties and create adult basic education programs for migrant farmworkers who had decided to relocate out of the fields and into Milwaukee.

With expanding programming and a growing number of staff, the UMOS board decided to purchase a building on Milwaukee's south side in 1968 to serve as headquarters and home for the organization's day-care program site. The relocation coincided with the expansion of adult education programming, now an intensive twenty-week set of courses at Milwaukee Technical College. These classes were geared toward displaced farmworkers who needed new skills to find work in urban areas. Enrollees took English classes and received instruction in arithmetic and job skills. Some students would go on to enroll in more schooling via the federal Manpower Development Training Act with hopes of learning trade-based skills. By the end of the 1968 harvest season, UMOS operated in thirty Wisconsin counties.

Despite the initial success of some UMOS programs, members of Wisconsin's Latino community pushed for more representation in leadership positions to have a voice in guiding UMOS's programs and priorities. Facing protests from Latino migrant counselors and community leaders, white members of the governing board resigned their positions in January 1969, transferring control to Latino leadership. To shepherd UMOS in its new direction, Jesus Salas became executive director in March 1969. Under the direction of the new board, UMOS began a reshaping of their staff and missions. Social workers who spoke only English were replaced with bilingual community workers, many of whom were of Mexican descent and had once been a part of the migrant stream to the state. The organization also set up self-help and advocacy groups capable of solving larger structural problems affecting migrants. Ultimately, UMOS hoped to offer former migrants the opportunity of self-determination in choosing employment and finding housing, as explained by Salas to the *Chicago Tribune*:

> It is really not so bad to be a migrant, if you can earn a decent life from it and if that is what you really want to do. It is no worse than being a plumber or a carpenter. The trouble is that my people do not have a choice. We want to give them a chance to be plumbers if they want to be plumbers, or carpenters if they want to be carpenters, or migrants if they want to be migrants, and have a decent life no matter what they choose, just like you or me.

Staff helped workers by relocating them to smaller towns such as Beaver Dam, Hartford, and Oshkosh instead of going to Milwaukee and Madison, which faced higher unemployment rates and a tightened housing market. Migrants found, however, that they weren't always welcomed in these smaller communities. While Spanish speakers didn't face active discrimination in finding apartments, Father John Maurice told the *Milwaukee Journal* he believed the "insidious nature of prejudice" prevented them from arranging living spaces comparable to those of their Anglo peers.

Over the next three decades UMOS has continued to advocate for migrant and Latino workers across the state. The nonprofit advocacy organization has grown to operate more than forty programs with more than twenty-five million dollars in grants from federal, state, and local funding sources. Under the leadership of directors Salvador Sanchez and Lupe Martinez, as well as countless staff and volunteers, the advocacy and service organization has expanded employment and educational opportunities, workplace protections, legislative advocacy, and connections between rural and urban Mexican Americans.

THE UNITED COMMUNITY CENTER

In Milwaukee, displaced farmworkers joined the Mexican and Mexican American industrial workers and business owners already inhabiting the city's south side, while others scattered throughout the Greater Milwaukee area as they searched for employment, equitable educational opportunities, and suitable housing. Tejanos joined the more than fifteen thousand Spanish speakers, including many Puerto Rican and Cuban transplants, living throughout southeastern Wisconsin's urban centers. As the Latino community in Milwaukee swelled, several organizations developed in the 1960s to serve them. Under the direction of Reverend Gil Marrero, the south side's Spanish Baptist Church collaborated with the Milwaukee Christian Center in 1963 to help address community concerns about Latino youth opportunities and a growing number of delinquent street gangs committing petty crimes. Marrero, a former pitcher for the Puerto Rican national baseball team who himself had been a member of a New York City street gang in his youth, had turned to a religious life by serving as a missionary in Central America before arriving in Milwaukee in 1962. The young pastor hoped to help Latino families "cut through the fog of prejudice" that fostered employment discrimination, antagonistic relations with the city's police, and unequal access to social aid benefits. With the help of Milwaukee Christian Center director Reverend Ken Smith, Marrero developed a program to reach the Spanish-speaking youth living in the core area of the south side, along with the ten thousand Spanish speakers in the Greater Milwaukee area.

Marrero first contacted a Spanish-speaking youth gang called the National Avenue Rebels operating within a few blocks of the church. The pastor hoped to redirect the Rebels' energy away from petty crime and street rumbles with rival gangs toward more productive endeavors. Marrero worked with the group's leaders, offering advice on how to elect officers democratically, create meeting rules, and collect weekly dues. With the help of the Baptist church and Mr. and Mrs. Marrero, the young members of the street gang transformed themselves into a community club newly dubbed the Thunderbirds.

The Christian Center's Latino outreach efforts grew into an independent program dubbed the Spot, which found a home in a small vacated tavern on Sixth Street. Teenage members of the Thunderbirds became involved in worship services and activities at the church while others attended the program's new vocational school. Working under the philosophy that programs needed to be tailored to meet the desires of participants, Marrero proposed a coffeehouse, a car repair club where youths could repair automobiles under the supervision of experienced mechanics, a beauty shop where students could learn fundamentals from trained beauticians, and other innovative programs. The Thunderbirds also took the initiative in expanding the center's physical fitness program, working together to repair and build much of the exercise equipment themselves. The center's boxing gym, run by former professional boxer Teddy Porter, covered about three thousand square feet of the site of a former hat factory on the east corner of South Sixth and West National Avenue. The gym trained amateurs, professionals, and Golden Glove aspirants including pro Vidal Flores and vaunted amateur middleweight Reynaldo Martinez. Fridays were always the busiest nights at the center, when area youths would gather after school to spend their afternoon boxing, weightlifting, and roller-skating and end their night with a dance. At the close of the festivities, the teenagers would gather as a group for a Thunderbirds business meeting and planning discussion under the guidance of Marrero to talk about neighborhood problems and engage in counseling services.

Under the leadership of Reverend Orlando Costas, a Puerto Rican–born pastor who assumed Marrero's position in late 1966, the freshly named United Spot continued to expand its community outreach efforts throughout the late 1960s. Costas and community members developed a center for job referrals, family counseling, and housing assistance. Staff even hired some of their more seasoned teenage members to go out into the neighborhood and look for children with nothing to do and no places to play, invite them to the center, and fold them into the Spot's activities. Dubbed the "pied pipers" program, this creative form of community youth work served to empower area teenagers to be leaders among their peers. In spite of these accomplishments, the Spot had to fight for continued funding, as legislators speaking to the *Milwaukee Journal* criticized it as a "haven for hoodlums" and a "gang hangout." Christian Center officials countered that one thousand teenagers, mostly Latinos, were now participating in its activities instead of loitering in the streets or becoming involved in antisocial behavior. The Christian Center's board of directors approved nearly $200,000 in emergency funds to keep it open, explaining that the United Spot had become "the only place in the entire city of Milwaukee that Latin American youth, and for that matter the Latin community in general, can truly call their own." The directors warned that without appropriate funding and support from the state, delinquency among Latino youth in the area would skyrocket and the city's Latino community would become further embittered and alienated from the larger Milwaukee community.

The community center declared itself independent from the Christian Center in 1970. Now under complete Latino community control and expanding its mission, the United Spot changed its name to the United Community Spot and then later to the United Community Center (UCC). It began to offer an alternative high school program and expanded its recreational, educational, and vocational programs. Throughout the ensuing decades, the facilities grew to include an alcohol and drug rehabilitation center, a renovated boxing gym, a community restaurant called Café El Sol, a senior citizen center, and an independent cultural and artistic center called Latino Arts, Incorporated. In the early 2000s, the UCC added a new teen center, a renovated auditorium and gallery for Latino Arts, Inc., and increased affordable housing options.

The UCC's commitment to bicultural education was solidified with the merger of local Bruce Guadalupe School in 1991. Originally the parochial school of Holy Trinity Catholic Church, Bruce Guadalupe had transitioned into a community school in 1970. With major input and involvement from parents, the school was reformulated in the belief that standardized educational programs could not meet the needs of all the pupils in the community, and with the goal of helping each student achieve fluency in both English and Spanish. Teachers, who were expected to be bilingual, stressed that children needed to be aware of their bicultural heritage. Originally only an elementary school, Bruce Guadalupe expanded to include kindergarten and middle school classes through the 1980s. The school faced financial difficulties throughout the 1970s and 1980s and was forced to move to a number of different sites, including buildings owned by St. John Cathedral High School, the St. Vincent de Paul Church, and St. Patrick's Church, before finding a permanent home at the UCC. Through contributions from foundations and independent donors, the UCC built a new building for the middle school in 2001.

THE COUNCIL FOR THE SPANISH SPEAKING AND THE SPANISH CENTER

The year 1963 proved to be fateful for community organizing in Milwaukee's Spanish-speaking community. Along with the Spot taking off, the Milwaukee Catholic Archdiocese formed the Archdiocesan Council for the Spanish Speaking to better coordinate services for transient migrants and the more than twenty-five thousand permanent Latinos in southeast Wisconsin. With representatives from Spanish-speaking nationalities in the area, the council set out to better meet the health, welfare, educational, employment, housing, and religious needs of the area's growing Latino population.

With help from other supportive community groups, the Archdiocesan Council for the Spanish Speaking opened El Centro Hispano Americano in May 1964. Also known as the Spanish Center, this was the first nonprofit organization managed in part by Latino leadership in Wisconsin. Under the direction of Reverend John Maurice, the center drew outreach workers from the Catholic Family Movement, Young Christian Workers, and college and high school students. For adults, the center provided recent arrivals with much-needed English classes, teaching rudimentary language skills to help them navigate the city and manage their money. The education program also offered a library for children and teenagers, along with a literacy program.

With demand for their services expanding throughout the decade, the Spanish Center seized upon newly available federal funding from the Office of Economic Opportunity in 1965. Program staff first applied for federal funds to start one of Wisconsin's first urban bilingual Head Start programs in the summer of 1965. When the nearby Our Lady of Guadalupe Catholic Church and Holy Trinity parish merged in 1966, the archdiocese gave the center use of the old Guadalupe Church and parish house at 230 West Washington as a permanent home for the Head Start program. The preschool classes proved so popular among the area's Spanish-speaking community that the Spanish Center decided to expand the curricular offerings to the entire school year. This expansion transformed the program into one of the neighborhood's first integrated and most successful schools with Latino, white, African American, and American Indian students in attendance.

While the Spanish Center focused on offering its Head Start program in its early years, staff and volunteers also pushed to incorporate innovate educational and health projects to meet broader community needs. Center staff expanded curricular offerings to include Adult Basic Education (ABE) classes funded by the State Board of Adult and Vocational Education and coordinated through Milwaukee Area Technical College, becoming within a few years the state's largest ABE program, led by program coordinator Jesus Pagan. The emphasis on one-on-one English-language tutoring helped Latino workers to develop job skills and helped push them out of the marginal jobs traditionally held by Spanish speakers. About four hundred completed the program, enabling them to move into jobs in industrial, service, and office work. A newly opened job referral office helped match Latino workers with job opportunities. With the encouragement of center staff, some even became entrepreneurs within the community, initiating a food buyer's club, a cooperative grocery store, and a people's craft shop.

As its educational offerings took off, the Spanish Center also offered other important services. In 1965, a local dentist recruited colleagues and dental hygienists to set up a free dental clinic in a small back room. The ad hoc staff began their clinic with an old dental chair and a retrofitted X-ray machine but later received donations from Marquette Dental School. The program offered Latino immigrants unprecedented access to basic dental care and has been so successful it continues to operate half a century later. Another program that had long-term success was a pediatric clinic set up by a Latino mothers group in the old Guadalupe rectory in 1969. With the help of volunteer doctors and nurses the makeshift medical services became a fully operational children's clinic known as the Guadalupe Center, serving Latinos throughout the south side for years to come.

Even as they gained better access to services, Latino workers struggled to find basic housing for themselves and their families, facing extreme difficulty in securing bank loans for home purchases. No bank served the neighborhood surrounding the Spanish Center, and if residents there ventured elsewhere, they struggled to provide the proof of income and other information required for a bank loan. The Spanish Center's board of directors identified this difficulty as a key barrier to economic advancement and established a credit union in 1966 to help alleviate the pressing problem of limited availability of credit for south-side Latinos. Organized under Office of Economic Opportunity guidelines to receive federal funding and support, the new credit union offered low-interest loans to its approximately 450 members, as well as budget counseling and advice for those seeking to grow their financial literacy. The newfound ability to purchase homes allowed the roots and investment of residents in their adopted community to grow and deepen.

At the center of this community El Centro—as the center was commonly called—had developed a vibrant community space with more than fourteen full-time workers, thirty part-time tutors, five neighborhood youth corps workers, and countless volunteers working on a variety of programs. Fund-raising dances with local bands at area churches helped fund the growing center and provide resources such as a bus to transport youth and adults to their classes.

As it grew, El Centro became more and more self-driven by the community it served. Like many of the other federal economic programs established in the mid- to late 1960s, the Spanish Center emphasized the hiring and training of community members to better build what directors referred to as "indigenous leadership." To create programming that truly served the city's Spanish speakers, the center gave priority to applicants from within the community to fill office and instructor positions. Through ad hoc apprenticeship schedules, new hires received training from existing staff and volunteers and learned on the job. Reverend Maurice, who understood that community members would know best how to serve Latinos in the area, stepped aside as director of the Council for the Spanish Speaking in 1970 and handed the reins to Carlos Sevilla, son of one of Milwaukee's *primeros*. The Spanish Center moved into its permanent home on National Avenue in 1978, a move that the center's director, Filberto Murguia, described to the *Milwaukee Journal* as "a dream, a small dream, but a dream come true."

"THE FUTURE OF BROWN AMERICANS"

As much as El Centro grew and changed in that time period, the community it served evolved even more drastically. With mechanization cutting labor needs in the fields surrounding larger metro areas, Mexican migrants had begun streaming into urban settings such as Milwaukee and Appleton. They sought higher-paying positions in industrial labor in the city, as well as more stable work that was not dependent on harvest seasons and annual migrations. The movement of Mexican workers to urban areas such as Milwaukee—called in-migration—was also accompanied by the development of other Latino communities in the city. These included a rapidly growing Puerto Rican community on the city's north and east sides and the arrival of a small group of refugees from Cuba following the Cuban Revolution in the early 1960s.

That Milwaukee was not dominated by one Latin-descent nationality set it apart from other American cities. Published reports estimated that around twenty thousand Latinos lived in the Milwaukee area in 1970, of which eleven thousand were either Mexican or Mexican American and the remaining nine thousand were Puerto Rican or of other Latin American descent. These communities were bound together not just by a common language and similar cultural heritages, but also by shared concerns over education, employment, housing, and ethno-racial discrimination. While geographic and national identity differences at times stood as barriers to full collaboration, Spanish-speaking communities emerged as a vocal and integral part of the city's civil rights movement and its call for full rights and participation in American political, economic, and social life.

In Milwaukee, Latinos of all national origins faced disparate economic and housing realities in comparison with the rest of the city. A 1969 study conducted by the Department of City Development classified nearly 7 percent of the residential units in the area as blighted, or deteriorated to the point of being uninhabitable, compared with a figure of 2 percent for the city as a whole. Employment specialists from WSES stationed at the Inner City Development Project on South Sixteenth Street estimated in 1970 that the unemployment rate on the near south side hovered around approximately 20 percent, while Milwaukee as a whole had 6 percent unemployment. Latinos also faced disproportionately higher rates of overcrowding (30 percent higher than the rest of the Milwaukee metropolitan area), and median property values that were 48 percent lower than those for other Milwaukeeans. In the 1960s, many Latinos had been forced to abandon their homes for the development of a new expressway system that ran over their south-side neighborhoods, contributing to the housing situation. In a meeting of the Governor's Coordinating Committee on Services to Minority Groups in Milwaukee in February 1966, Spanish-speaking residents complained that city officials were not aware of or attuned to the problems Latinos faced. Due in part to language barriers, community members complained that Spanish speakers faced subtle discrimination in employment, housing, and education that was often difficult to document.

Once again, Latino workers organized—but this time their focus had shifted from meeting short-term needs to making long-term progress on integrating more fully into American society. As this movement took hold in Milwaukee and other cities experiencing this sea change, the struggle was championed in the halls of Congress by Senator Gaylord Nelson of Wisconsin. In July 1969, Nelson rose on the floor of the US Senate to deliver an address titled "The Future of 'Brown Americans.'" Nelson, who served as the chairman of the Senate Subcommittee on Employment, Poverty, and Migratory Labor, warned his colleagues that Mexican Americans were "tired of waiting to be granted their full and unqualified rights as American citizens." The senator compared the situation of Mexican Americans to that of African Americans fighting for their civil rights, stressing that society and government's failure to rectify larger economic, social, and political problems had led to "racial bitterness, violence, and a growing polarization of the races." Nelson urged Congress to heed the cries of Mexican Americans, numbering more than five million across the United States, who currently occupied "one of the very lowest economic rungs on the ladder of American society."

Recounting the mounting educational disadvantages and economic deprivation Spanish speakers faced throughout the country, Nelson warned that "young Mexican-Americans [would not be] as willing as their parents to accept poverty and discrimination." Rising ferment among activists crying "brown power" at demonstrations marked a growing militancy, an aggressiveness that Nelson warned without government action would lead to riots and further polarization. The senator recounted how in Wisconsin, young Mexican Americans were beginning to organize against "poor housing, dead-end jobs, and political power-lessness." This new wave of activism pushed back against the "spirit of paternalism and charity" of "well-meaning people" to demand self-determination and respect for community and culture. Nelson ended his speech with a warning for his fellow congressmen: "We cannot have two societies—one black, one white. We cannot certainly have three societies—one black, one brown, one white. To break these barriers, to heal this division, to lead these longstanding Americans into the full rights and responsibilities of citizenship, is one of the urgent challenges facing this Nation."

✿❧

CHICANO SOCIAL ACTIVISM

Senator Nelson was right to recognize a generational shift in the ways in which some people of Mexican descent identified themselves and their place in larger American society, a newly emerging identity and social justice cause known as the Chicano Movement. Those who identified as Chicanos felt a deep pride in their cultural heritage and wanted to end discrimination against people of Mexican descent rather than learn to cope with it. Chicanos critiqued older mutual aid societies for celebrating Mexican cultural achievements without confronting larger economic disadvantages and social prejudice facing Latinos. Many harshly disapproved of organizations that advocated assimilation and integration as the only path to full American rights and citizenship. Chicanos' anger at racism and discrimination in the United States often led them to adopt more confrontational strategies such as sit-ins, direct action protests, and marches to push for wholesale societal change.

While fighting for economic and political justice, members of the Chicano Movement also created a rich cultural movement through art, theater, dance, and song. Milwaukeean Juan Alvarez, a twenty-three-year-old artist and Vietnam War veteran who grew up in Texas and Mexico, found an outlet for his Chicanismo through murals on the theme on which he had devoted his life: "la raza," an expression of pride in Mexican culture and heritage. Painted on the walls of buildings throughout the south side of Milwaukee, Alvarez's murals emphasized Chicano pride while drawing upon the tradition of renowned Mexican muralists like Diego Rivera and José Orozco, whose art was concerned with improving the lot of the people they immortalized in Mexico. Alvarez explained that the phrase "la raza," which had become a rallying cry for Chicanos throughout the United States, defined every aspect of his art and social activism: "To me, it means my people, especially the underprivileged, those who in Mexico are called 'los de abajo' (those on the bottom). It is an emotion that I feel. I will keep doing and working for my people until their problems are solved. I have given all myself to this—la raza."

Throughout the period, Chicano activists worked to coordinate their social activism with the city's African American and Puerto Rican communities fighting for similar causes. Many of the issues the Chicano community faced during the 1960s and 1970s were similar to the grievances of contemporary social movements. Like African American civil rights activists such as the NAACP Young Commandos under the guidance of Father James Groppi, Latinos in Milwaukee fought for control of programs that affected housing, education, health, and economic opportunities as well as equal access to voting and political representation. Chicano protestors joined African American civil rights activists in 1968 to fight for fair hiring practices at one of Milwaukee's iconic corporations, the Allen-Bradley Company. Members of the Young Commandos noted that of the company's six thousand employees, only twenty-five were African American and only fourteen were Latino. Union leaders from the United Electrical, Radio, and Machine Workers Local 1111 requested a sit-down meeting with Allen-Bradley management to insert a clause in their contract prohibiting discrimination against minorities. The Commandos organized a rally and pickets, while Groppi held a Mass in support of the union's efforts. Latino leaders such as UMOS area coordinator Armando Orellana, representing a new community advocacy group called the Latin American Community, joined them. The coalition insisted that Allen-Bradley hire enough black workers to equal 12 percent of its workforce as well as enough Mexican and Puerto Rican workers to equal 5 percent of its workforce. At a meeting of more than one hundred fifty Spanish speakers at the Guadalupe Center, Orellana argued that Allen-Bradley's expansion into the city's near south side was taking away the homes of Latinos without offering them the opportunity for employment. Reverend Orlando Costas of the Evangelical Baptist Church added that the Latino coalition should join the NAACP's protests and "be ready to respond to whatever the situation calls for." In anticipation of direct action against the company, Spanish-speaking volunteers received training from the Commandos in peaceful protest tactics.

In response to the pickets and the ensuing negative media attention, Allen-Bradley agreed to scrap a policy that prioritized the hiring of friends and relatives of employees. This proved to be the only concession management offered, as they were unwilling to insert antidiscrimination language into the employee contract or actively recruit minority workers. Finding the hiring agreement piecemeal and unacceptable, Groppi and the demonstrators returned to the picket line in August 1969, now more militant and intent on achieving their aims. Borrowing from Black Power activists, young Latinos in attendance wore brown berets with buttons on their headwear identifying them as members of the Milwaukee Latin American Youth Organization, later known as the Brown Berets. The youth were joined by community leaders including Assemblyman Lloyd Barbee, executive director of the Milwaukee Urban League Wesley Scott, Alderwoman Vel Phillips, and UMOS director Jesus Salas.

The Allen-Bradley fight led to the creation of a new organization called the Latin American Union for Civil Rights (LAUCR). Under the direction of Orellana, Ernesto Chacón, Avelardo "Lalo" Valdez, Roberto Hernandez, and Juan Alvarez, LAUCR worked directly with Latino community members on strategies to build what members referred to as a "viable Latin community" for Milwaukee. Organizers conducted community-wide surveys to explore the concerns and priorities of Spanish speakers in Milwaukee. These conversations led LAUCR to organize around several issues, including police harassment and discrimination against Latinos; the need for a bilingual/bicultural school; harassment by immigration officials; better access to health services; discriminatory hiring practices at local companies such as Pabst Brewing; and budget cuts in social service programs. The organization helped stage a walkout of more than one hundred Milwaukee high school students in September 1969 who demanded more Spanish-speaking teachers, more Latin American history in regular history courses, and Spanish-speaking counselors. Members of LAUCR also began publishing a monthly newspaper called *La Guardia* in 1969. Staffed by volunteers and working with donated equipment, *La Guardia* ("the guard" or "the watch" in Spanish) was an explicitly radical Chicano newspaper working to fill a void in press coverage of the state's Spanish-speaking community.

Contributor John Torres described news coverage in the city as being "crisis oriented," which meant that it usually took "a crisis situation, such as a shooting, bombing, or some type of protest to get the news media into the Latino community." The paper's editorial board hoped to preserve the community's native language while promoting Latin American culture and creating awareness in young Latinos of their cultural heritage. News stories kept Latinos abreast of "Brown Power" issues across the country and Latin America, including anti–Vietnam War protests, police brutality concerns, and revolutionary efforts in Puerto Rico. *La Guardia* also provided volunteers to the Centro Cultural Educativo Chicano Boricua, a community-based high school where staff conducted workshops in cinema, photography, and writing and began a film series and community theater group.

Besides LAUCR, other Latino Milwaukee organizations stepped in to advocate for improved bilingual and bicultural education for the city's Spanish-speaking students. Milwaukee's Spanish-speaking community charged the public school system with "anti-Latin bias" in a letter penned to the federal civil rights commission in 1968. Citing a high dropout rate among Spanish-surnamed children, the lack of Spanish-surnamed teachers, and a shortage of textbooks covering the contributions of Latinos to the country, the community demanded that Latinos "be given an equal opportunity to an adequate education in Milwaukee." Led by community members such as Ponce Renteria and Dante Navarro, the Mexican-American Political and Educational Committee (MAPEC) worked with other Latino organizations and church leaders to develop experimental bilingual programs at schools with large Spanish-speaking populations, including Vieau and Holy Trinity Elementary Schools and South Division and Lincoln High Schools. MAPEC's advocacy prompted the Milwaukee Public Schools to start early bilingual and bicultural education throughout the district in 1969. The district hired Latinas from the community to serve as the city's first bicultural aides, bringing a wealth of experience with them to share with their students. Many of the aides were mothers whose thirst for knowledge and education was rekindled by their time in the classroom with their students, prompting them to take college courses and earn degrees to build their own skills.

Latinos also banded together to press local and state politicians to live up to their promises of serving the most impoverished citizens of the state through equal access to welfare benefits. The Unión Beneficia Hispana, a Latino welfare rights and housing advocacy organization, pushed for the Milwaukee welfare department to provide Spanish-speaking caseworkers and bilingual forms for Latino families. Unión president Ted Uribe, a former air force medic and welfare recipient, explained to state legislators that recent budget cuts to the welfare program had made being poor even more difficult for Latino Wisconsinites as parents struggled to provide food and warm clothing for their families. Unión members such as Clementia Castro worked to educate the Latino community about their right to social services, stating, "When you learn your rights, you feel more free; and you're not afraid." Activists such as Castro and Uribe believed that in the richest country in the world, people deserved access to decent housing and living conditions.

The Latino community found allies among Wisconsin's African American civil rights activists in their fight against state cuts to social service and welfare benefits. The two communities joined together for a seven-day welfare march from Milwaukee to Madison in September 1969. Led by mothers and their children and supported by Father Groppi, Jesus Salas, clergy, and students, the marchers hoped their protest would halt cuts to welfare benefits and social service agencies proposed by legislators in an upcoming special legislative session. Wearing buttons stating "I Support Guaranteed Adequate Income for All Americans" and "Welfare Rights Now," Chicano and African American protesters entered the state capitol and occupied the Assembly chambers, disrupting the start of the session with cries of "power to the people." Although the protests were ultimately unsuccessful in stopping the budget cuts, Latino and African American activists demonstrated their ability to organize communities to fight for social change.

In 1971, Ted Uribe helped organize Esperanza Unida, a nonprofit economic development program that helped unemployed workers, many of them disabled, learn marketable skills and access unemployment and workmen's compensation. Esperanza Unida also facilitated clothing and food drives for the neediest in the Spanish-speaking community throughout the early 1970s. Under the leadership of director Richard Oulahan, the organization combatted racism, immigration problems, and tactics by employers, physicians, and insurance carriers who created hardships for Latinos injured on the job throughout the Milwaukee area. In 1984, Esperanza Unida expanded into a job retraining center, offering courses in Spanish and English and in work fields ranging from automobile repair to housing rehab, child care, and many others. Funded through state and federal grants, these programs were unique in that they didn't require their students to have a high school diploma, fluency in English, or funds to pay for their courses, three barriers that often stood in the way of Latinos finding new work or furthering their job skills.

CHICANAS ADELANTE! WOMEN IN THE CHICANO MOVEMENT

Perhaps no community activist connected the different generations of Mexican and Chicano advocacy as much as Juanita Renteria. Born in Illinois in 1914, Renteria moved to Milwaukee in 1937 where she met her husband, Ponciano, one of *los primeros* in the city. Renteria used her bilingual skills to interpret for Spanish speakers at places such as the courthouse throughout the 1940s, 1950s, and 1960s. By the early 1970s, she noted that her time in the community was divided between helping serve Mexican migrant workers and urban residents. Her passion for community advocacy drew her to several different projects and positions, including helping establish UMOS, where she served as its assistant director; working as a vocational counselor for Latino youth at the Spanish Center; directing the senior center La Guadalupana; and running unsuccessfully for the Milwaukee County School Board. Renteria also joined numerous political and social justice organizations such as the Mexican-American Political Education Committee, Centro Nuestro, LULAC, the United States Commission on Civil Rights, LAUCR, the Governor's Commission for the Spanish Speaking, the Mental Health Planning Council of Milwaukee County, and the Women's Political Caucus. The veteran of countless marches and protests hoped to align the efforts of these groups, arguing that they could accomplish more together. "We should get the community to become more sophisticated politically," Renteria told the *Milwaukee Sentinel* in 1977. "We should teach the community to progress by becoming more involved in the political system." She viewed herself as a broker between the city's Latino community and the general population, noting that she was "tired of the stereotypes that the larger community has of us as a poor, uneducated

group of citizens. I would like to erase that picture of us as always hold-
ing out an outreached hand."

Along with her advocacy efforts on behalf of the state's Spanish-
speaking communities, Renteria also joined Milwaukee Latina activists
throughout the 1960s and 1970s in speaking out for expanded women's
rights. Through her work in Chicano organizations, Renteria had identified a "machismo problem" in the Spanish-speaking community as
women struggled to gain equal footing not just in economic settings, but
in their homes and in social justice organizations as well. Renteria explained her concern that Latina mothers "will work very hard and sacri-
fice much so that the children get a good education," and yet were
frequently excluded from important decision-making processes. Her as-
sessment was part of a growing critique by Latinas called Chicana fem-
inism, a movement within a movement that understood the fight for
equal rights for Chicanos and women as being interconnected.

Latina activists took the fight for equal gender rights to their own organizations in the 1970s. In 1971, Latinas created the Power of Women
(POW)-Fuerza Femenina coalition to fight against a "macho cult in
Latino culture" as well as for greater representation at the city's LAUCR-
organized Latino Conference. The coalition organizers described their
objective to the *Milwaukee Journal* as a "polite war" against the "super
male who traditionally has been the sole breadwinner, money handler
and decision maker of the Latin family." Led by Gloria Salas,
Clementina Castro, Mary Lou Massignani, and Irasema Flores, the sixty-
member female caucus presented a list of their demands to the citywide
conference, asserting that women felt that for too long they had been rel-
egated to "cooking tortillas." Addressing the men in the audience, Gloria
Salas stated, "It's hypocritical to talk about Latin power without also
meaning the power of Latin women." Their demands included recognition of their caucus, as well as leadership positions for Latinas on all
boards of directors for agencies and organizations serving the Latino
community. Activists such as Esmeralda Cruz believed that to be truly
free, the Chicano community need to recognize the changing gender
dynamics in society and at home: "I feel very liberated. I feel I'm making
my stand for women's liberation—as well as for my people's liberation—
by making my stand for my people as a woman."

WHI IMAGE ID 92280

Led by Jesus Salas and Salvador Sanchez, thirty members of Obreros Unidos march from Wautoma to Madison to petition lawmakers to hold farms and food industry corporations accountable for better working conditions for migrant farm workers. Two men in the middle of the march hold signs that say, "Juntarnos para ser reconocidos. Hablar para ser oidos. La raza tiene causa" ("Join us to be recognized. Speak to be heard. The race has cause.").

WHI IMAGE ID 11909

Shirley Mecha, a teacher at Meadow Brook School in Manitowoc, helps migrant students use resources in the classroom library in 1961.

Courtesy of Guadalupe Macias

The Nacho Zaragoza y Orquestra Sensacional performs in the 1960s.

WHI IMAGE ID 91647

A family of migrant workers from Texas is pictured near their tempoary home in Waushara County in 1967.

WHI IMAGE ID 92289

Children of migrant worker families play a ball game in a circle at a Waushara County Labor Camp. Around them are buildings that served as temporary housing for migrant farm workers.

WHI IMAGE ID 91911

Migrant farm workers meet in Bancroft after a 1967 strike organized by Obreros Unidos, an independent farm worker labor union in the 1960s

WHI IMAGE ID 93067

Piles of *La Voz Mexicana* (the Mexican voice) await distribution at the Wautoma office of Obreros Unidos labor union in 1969. The headline refers to the cannery workers' union contract with Libby's Hartford plant.

Two boys distribute copies of *La Voz Mexicana*, the official newspaper of the Obreros Unidos farm workers' union. They are standing near a movie theater featuring Spanish-language films. On the marquee, the film *El Llanero* ("The Cowboy") is advertised.

WHI IMAGE ID 93076

Obreros Unidos demonstrators paint signs at a Milwaukee rally in 1969.

Matias Perez and her daughter empty buckets of cucumbers picked into burlap bags on a farm in Wautoma in 1970.

WHI IMAGE ID 25046

Children participating in programs at La Raza, Inc., a migrant nonprofit social organization in Appleton founded in 1970.

WHI IMAGE ID 128226

From the Archives Department, University of Wisconsin–Milwaukee Libraries

A University of Wisconsin–Milwaukee official speaks with protesters occupying the chancellor's office during the August 1970 demonstrations leading to the establishment of the Spanish Speaking Outreach Institute.

Althea Dotzour Photography

Luz Celedón, a first-grade teacher at Nuestro Mundo Community School in Madison, was named the Wisconsin Bilingual Teacher of the Year in 2014.

WHI IMAGE ID 129784

Thousands marched in Milwaukee for immigrant rights on May 1, 2006, also known as May Day.

CHICANO CAMPUS ACTIVISM

Chicano protests for fair employment standards, improved social services, and reformed police departments helped inspire university students on campuses throughout Wisconsin in the 1970s. Chicano students joined with black and American Indian activist organizations on University of Wisconsin campuses to fight for ethnic studies departments and better recruitment and retention programs for minority students. Their activism, which often coincided with antiwar, feminist, and labor protests, spurred the creation of Chicano studies initiatives at a number of campuses across the state.

In Milwaukee, education activists strived to create a department attuned to the city's Latino students at the University of Wisconsin–Milwaukee. Following their work organizing high school students, members of the Latin American Union for Civil Rights helped form the Council for Education of Latin Americans (CELA). This organization worked to improve Latinos' access to the University of Wisconsin–Milwaukee and to develop community education programs. Later, CELA would attempt to "Latinize" university institutions to provide educational opportunities for young Latinos across Milwaukee. Members of CELA proposed the Spanish Speaking Outreach Institute (SSOI), a program that would better serve Latinos as well as push the campus to live up to its mission as an urban university focused on helping to alleviate urban problems. Mexican and Puerto Rican students and community members banded together throughout 1970 to force university leadership to meet with them to negotiate the terms for building the SSOI. Because the creation of such a program necessitated coordination and funding from various schools and departments on campus, activists such as Roberto Hernández, Ernesto Chacón, Jesus Salas, and Margo Anderson attempted to negotiate directly with the Office of the Chancellor to garner any sort of support for their plan. Finding administration to be resistant to their demands, more than two hundred CELA members and allies borrowed techniques from other Chicano protests occurring in universities across the country. They staged sit-ins, protests, and campouts at the office of Chancellor J. Martin Klotsche. Willing to face arrests and even expulsion for their actions, the students were ultimately successful in

November 1970, when the school opened the Spanish Speaking Outreach Institute to serve Milwaukee's Latino population.

The establishment of SSOI marked a victory for Milwaukee's Latino community on a number of fronts. The activism leading to the center's creation united Spanish speakers of different nationalities under a concrete goal to improve educational access for the city's Latino population. The efforts to hold a public university accountable to its community's citizens also demonstrated the efficacy of direct action by young activists, refueling calls for more sit-ins, pickets, and protests. This sense of activism was emboldened by the activists' experience with prior federal programs administered in the city, which emphasized community control and input in the creation, direction, and maintenance of publicly funded programming. After decades of advocacy by students and community members, the University of Wisconsin–Milwaukee in 1996 established a Latino-focused program and hub called the Roberto Hernández Center, named in honor of the late former CELA leader.

Besides Milwaukee, the children of migrant workers who had permanently settled in areas such as Wautoma, Appleton, and Fond du Lac and had begun attending the University of Wisconsin–Oshkosh in the early 1970s found their own activist voices. Joining together to form an organization they called Chicanos Unidos in 1971, students submitted a proposal to administration and the Board of Regents with a list of demands that included more concerted efforts to recruit Chicano students, a dedicated adviser for Spanish speakers, and more robust funding opportunities. Most radically, the students called for the purchase of a residence hall for Spanish-speaking students to be called "La Casa" and the establishment of a Chicano cultural center within the new home. Chicanos hoped the residence would allow them to achieve academic success without the social and economic barriers wrought by institutional discrimination they faced in the dormitories and surrounding town. Chicanos Unidos achieved a partial victory when the university established a multicultural center for all minority students on campus in 1972. The organization would later coordinate and sponsor La Raza Month in April 1973, which included art shows, political debates, and rallies and an appearance by national Chicano activist Rodolfo "Corky" Gonzales. The organization expanded its mission to include precollege access for Chicanos, as members visited Wisconsin high schools to recruit Chicano students to UW–Oshkosh and serve as role models for young students who might not have considered college an option for their future. Like students at University of Wisconsin campuses across the state, Chicanos at Oshkosh also coordinated boycotts of local grocery stores that sold California lettuce and grape products from growers engaged in labor disputes with César Chávez's United Farm Workers.

The successful petitioning for a Chicano/Latino studies program at the University of Wisconsin–Milwaukee and Oshkosh prompted students at other UW schools to push for similar departments. After months of attempting to convince administrators through meetings proved unproductive, University of Wisconsin–Madison students began picketing for a Chicano Studies Department in the spring of 1974. With administrators unwilling to commit funding for an ethnic studies department, Chicano students from around the state went directly to the Joint Finance Committee of the state legislature to secure $50,000 for "American Ethnic Studies" programming at the Madison, Milwaukee, and Whitewater campuses. Throughout 1975, Madison Chicano students organized under the banner of La Raza Unida Party picketed South Hall for weeks, demanding that E. David Cronon, dean of the College of Letters and Science, create an independent department for the study of Chicano history, culture, and language. They also called for expanded admittance and scholarship support for Chicano students to the university. In 1975, only 228 Spanish-surnamed undergraduate and graduate students were enrolled at the campus, and of that small number, only thirty students were Chicanos. As in Milwaukee, Madison students created rotating picket lines and occupied Cronon's office, tactics that sometimes led to the arrest of students. The protests came to an end in the late summer of 1975 when Chancellor Edwin Young agreed to hire a Chicano scholar to develop a Chicano Studies Department, leading to the establishment of the campus's first Chicano Studies program through the School of Education in 1976.

While Chicano Studies programs in Milwaukee, Oshkosh, and Madison came into existence because of student protesting and picketing, administrators at the University of Wisconsin–Whitewater were more proactive in reaching out to Chicano students and striving for cultural inclusiveness. Professors in the counseling and developmental psychology departments first began outreach to Chicano high school students in the Whitewater and Kenosha areas in 1968 through bilingual programs that aimed to link the children of migrant workers to a collegiate experience. In the early 1970s, the campus's academic affairs program created a tutoring system developed with an eye toward the recruitment and retention of minority students. Academic and social counseling aimed to provide a welcoming home away from home for Chicano students to avoid alienation, while instructional centers focused on reading and writing skills with one-on-one coaching and mentoring. Throughout the early and mid-1970s the Whitewater campus welcomed growing cohorts of black, Chicano, and American Indian students to their campus.

Despite the successes of student activists at University of Wisconsin campuses across the state in the early 1970s, Chicano students continued to fight for committed resources like faculty positions, scholarships, and departmental support throughout the last decades of the twentieth century. Student organizations such as Movimiento Estudiantil Chicano de Aztlán (MEChA, or Chicano Student Movement for Aztlán) served as cultural homes for many Chicano students who felt alienated on college campuses, and organized students to continue to push administrators for dedicated funding, more robust curricular offerings, and plans to retain Chicanos who had earned admittance to their university. The continual call for a financial commitment to Chicano and ethnic studies prompted Governor Lee Dreyfus to recommend that the University of Wisconsin–Superior be converted into a Spanish-speaking campus as a radical solution to stem enrollment declines in 1980. While Dreyfus's plan met opposition from legislators and some student groups—including those who feared such a plan would drain resources from the Milwaukee and Madison campuses—such efforts represented the efficacy of Chicano activism for committed resources to culturally relevant education.

GROWING MEXICAN AMERICAN COMMUNITIES ACROSS SOUTHEAST WISCONSIN

The 1970 census marked rapidly changing demographics in cities and towns across Wisconsin, as more Latinos made their way to urban areas with better-paying employment opportunities. At the start of the decade, the State Employment Service estimated that more than fifty thousand people of Latin American descent lived in Wisconsin, with more than half of those people living in the Milwaukee area and the rest spread among smaller communities throughout the state. In Kenosha, more than five thousand Spanish speakers developed cultural and social spaces for themselves throughout the decade, including a Latin American Center at St. James Catholic Church under the direction of Reverend Roberto Rodriguez. Mexican Americans gathered every year at the church to celebrate fiestas commemorating Our Lady of Guadalupe, where children wearing traditional Mexican clothing marched with members of the Cristo Rey Society in a grand procession bearing the statue of the Virgin of Guadalupe. Community members also gathered to commemorate Mexican Independence Day with a festival that included dances, the selection of a festival queen, speeches, and a Mass honoring the dead heroes who fought for national independence. Reverend Rodriguez commented that the Chicano "minority, more than any other, has served as a catalyst here in the US toward the acceptance of cultural diversity as necessary for the creation of a more democratic society."

Kenosha's growing Latino community also rushed to meet several economic and social issues developing in their community throughout the decade. Cuts to federal funding for social services, job training, and bilingual education programs exacerbated rising unemployment, language difficulties, and hiring discrimination. Organizations such as UMOS and a local La Raza Unida branch lent their support as best they could in offering basic education for adults, vocational programs, and counseling and employment services but suffered from a similar scarcity in resources. Many Mexican Americans also struggled to enter even entry-level industrial work. Vidal Rodriguez, employed with the Job Opportunity Services and a member of the La Raza Unida, criticized Kenosha's larger corporations, such as the American Motor Company, Snap-on

Tools, and Eaton Dynamic, for hiring only a minimal number of Latinos to barely meet federal employment standards.

While most of Kenosha's Spanish speakers worked in low-paying factory jobs, an upcoming younger generation hoped that expanded educational access would help them obtain better-paying positions. Families allied with La Sociedad de Padres Latinos (Society of Latino Parents) advocated for bilingual education and the maintenance and celebration of Latino culture in public schools in hopes of stemming the growing dropout rate among Latino adolescents. Parents such as Luis González, a native of Guadalajara who had come to the United States to find a better job at the American Motors Company, didn't believe complete assimilation into American society was possible or even ideal for Mexican Americans, and instead hoped that his children could "learn to be (North) Americans but . . . also want to retain what we have." Luis and his wife, Blanca, spoke Spanish to their children at home with the hope that they would grow up to be bilingual and appreciate "the beauty of Latin culture" while striving for a better life in Wisconsin.

Many in Racine's growing Mexican American community had once been migrant workers who could trace their history of traveling to Wisconsin back to the 1940s. Their families had made the decision to settle in the city to find more stable employment in foundries and factories in the area. With financial support from the Milwaukee Catholic Archdiocese, Mexican American and Puerto Rican community members founded the Racine Spanish Center in 1968. Serving around eight thousand people of Mexican descent and an additional 250 Puerto Ricans in the area, the center offered bilingual classes in topics ranging from nutrition to drivers' education, facilitated a youth organization, and ran a breakfast program. It also became a familiar space for the city's Latinos to discuss community problems in housing, employment, and education and organize for change. Many of the people who served on the center's board of directors had previous experience working at other Latino advocacy organizations, such as UMOS, LULAC, and MAPEC. The biggest celebration of the year for Racine's Latino community, as it was for many others across the state, were always the Masses celebrating Our Lady of Guadalupe and the parties that followed at St. Patrick's Church. Often officiated by Milwaukee Archbishop William Cousins and assisted by Spanish-speaking priests from the Racine and Milwaukee areas, the celebration included an ornate procession led by a Guadalupe float created by students at Washington Park High School and accompanied by the Guadalupe Children's Choir and mariachi groups.

The 1970 census recorded that the Spanish-speaking population in Waukesha had grown to about 3,200 people, representing nearly 8 percent of the city's total population and accounting for the area's largest minority community. With the Spanish-speaking community growing and their needs mounting, a coalition of white Waukesha community members formed History Builders, Incorporated, with startup funds from the United Way to concentrate outreach and aid efforts to Latinos. The organization first purchased a house on Ryan Street in the heart of the Mexican community, where it operated a day-care program. Over time more Spanish speakers became involved in the center's day-to-day activities, until Latino leaders took the reins of leadership and rebranded the organization La Casa de Esperanza (the House of Hope). It became a principal advocate for educational, economic, and social opportunities for Waukesha's Latino community.

La Casa's leadership joined with the Latino community in 1973 to voice continued frustrations with the Waukesha public schools and their inability to serve Spanish-speaking students. Although repeated requests for expanded services had prompted the board of education to introduce bilingual and bicultural education in 1969, a small staff and limited resources restricted the effectiveness of the program. Protests erupted when the district passed over a bilingual candidate to fill a guidance counselor vacancy. One community leader explained to the local press, "The fuse has been burning a long time. Now it's run out, and hit the dynamite." With support from La Casa, Latino students organized a boycott and ten-day walkout to protest continual insensitivity to the needs of Latino students in early 1973. Responses from the white community were less than supportive. In a letter to the *Waukesha Daily Freeman*, one resident suggested that if Latinos were dissatisfied with the city's public schools, "They should go back from whence they came," while others accused minority groups of not doing enough to assimilate into the larger society. Despite the Latino community's continued efforts to increase funding and resources for the bilingual program, the Waukesha school district initiated a freeze on the hiring of bilingual staff in 1975.

Undeterred by these setbacks, Waukesha's Mexican American leaders continued to push for broader access to political, social, educational, and economic avenues. Oscar Sánchez, a longtime Waukesha resident, served on the school board from 1973 to 1978, first as an appointed member and then as an elected representative. María García San Miguel Benavides, who had helped found Escuela Preparatoria para Niños (Preparatory School for Children) in the mid-1960s, directed its growth after a merger with La Casa de Esperanza in 1975. La Casa executive director Pedro Rodriguez also took the fight for Spanish-speaking students to the statehouse, testifying to the Senate Subcommittee on Education in support of a statewide bilingual education bill in 1974.

By the end of the 1970s, Waukesha's Latino community had grown to more than five thousand members, making up about a tenth of the city's total population. Successful advocacy work by La Casa de Esperanza, along with the Waukesha Equal Opportunity Commission and St. Joseph's Catholic Church, continued to combat discrimination in employment and social spaces throughout the city. El Día de la Comunidad/Latino Community Day program also brought together Waukesha's different Latino ethnic communities for a march through Waukesha and daylong celebration for the entire city.

NEW MEXICAN AMERICAN COMMUNITIES ACROSS THE STATE

Unlike in southeastern Wisconsin, the Mexican community in Madison was still rather small by the late 1960s. The first Latinos to arrive in Dane County were college students from Mexico and other Latin American countries who arrived early in the twentieth century. By 1970, however, the census counted only 2,600 Spanish-speaking persons living in Dane County. By 1976 that number had more than doubled and was expected to grow even larger as more Mexicans settled out of the agricultural migrant worker stream and into industrial cities. Of the growing Latino population, about 65 percent were Americans of Mexican descent, many of whom continued to have connections with family members and friends still working as migrant laborers in surrounding fields. Community and social service organizations rushed to better serve the growing Mexican American community. The federally funded Organización de Hispano-Americanos, one of the city's first agencies created to cater to Spanish speakers, developed early English-language programming with aid from local community colleges, while the city's Catholic archdiocese established an office to serve the growing community. Employment specialists at the Madison office of UMOS worked with newly arrived migrant workers to supply financial assistance and permanent work in the city, while at the University of Wisconsin–Madison, students such as Maria Anita Sánchez, a journalism student and herself a former migrant, developed bilingual newsletters that offered insight into the often lonely existence of resettled migrants. Gladys Benavides Corbit, an Equal Opportunities investigator for the city of Madison, identified a growing effort within the Latino community to confront local institutions to be more responsive to Spanish speakers. "The Madison community will hear more and more from the Latin community now and they'll hear about it in an organized manner," she told the *Capital Times* in 1971.

Chicanos and other Spanish speakers struggled to develop their own space within the state's capital city, especially as it pertained to education. At the University of Wisconsin–Madison, Mexican American students formed an organization called La Academia de la Raza along with community members to facilitate dialogues between Chicanos and the larger Dane County population. The *Capital Times* columnists Pancho Oyarbide and Salvadore Usabel noted that the Madison school system, "recognized as one of the most progressive and sensitive in the state," had offered very little to the hundreds of Chicano and Latino students in the district. They cited a lack of bilingual education programs as a contributing factor for rising dropout rates among Chicano youth. The Latino community continued to apply pressure upon the school district to hire bilingual staff throughout the late 1970s and 1980s. Public school educators such as Deborah Gil Casado, Anita Sandoval, and Elena Chavez-Mueller helped students navigate their identities as both Latinos and Americans, and in the process helped raise the graduation rate of Spanish-speaking high school seniors. Student groups such as LUCHA (the word for struggle in Spanish) also provided extracurricular spaces for Latino high school students to navigate their Latino heritage and study their cultural history.

By the early 1970s, approximately seventy Mexican American families had settled in Fond du Lac, with hundreds more living in the surrounding rural areas. Many of the families had once been part of the migrant labor stream but had decided to stay in Fond du Lac to find what mother Angelina Macias described as "a better future" for their children.

To serve the growing community, Fond du Lac County in 1971 used federal funding to hire a director for Mexican American counseling. This position was responsible for locating Mexican American families and aiding them in acquiring employment, acquainting them with local resources, and referring them to the appropriate social service agencies. The Mexican-American Project of Fond du Lac, founded in 1972, sponsored community dances with Latino music, with all proceeds going to assist Spanish-speaking persons in the area. Mexican American community members also pushed local social service agencies to hire Spanish-speaking staff while also working with Spanish instructors at Marian College to improve community members' English skills.

Industrial work helped Sheboygan become a destination for Mexican American migration in the early 1970s. Before 1970, only a small handful of Spanish speakers called the city home. Tejanos such as Belisario Cappetillo and Jim Sánchez had first settled in the city in the 1950s to work at companies such as Armour Leather, and often found the city less than hospitable to Mexican Americans. Early settlers faced difficulties in discrimination from restaurants and bars, in finding housing, and in securing equal treatment from the city's law enforcement. They found the environment more amenable to Spanish speakers with the arrival of more Mexicans in the 1970s, however, as Sánchez told the *Sheboygan Press* in 1970, "People don't stare anymore, you don't see so many necks twisting. A lot of doors have started to open."

By 1970, about three hundred Mexican Americans had settled in Sheboygan, most of whom had been migrant workers. The former pickers and canners in the city were connected by what the *Sheboygan Press* referred to as "a past of hard labor, low pay, and lots of traveling" as well as a hopeful "future of good jobs and good money." Tejanos such as Manuel Martínez left migrant labor that paid the state's minimum wage of $1.30 an hour for industrial jobs at the Kohler Company that paid more than $4 an hour. Newly arrived families, however, experienced difficulties in securing affordable housing and initially struggled to establish a cultural space in the city, and turned to local groups such as St. Vincent de Paul, the Salvation Army, and the Sheboygan Human Rights Association for aid. A recently opened UMOS office in Sheboygan identified the city as a long-sought-for answer to the problem of overpopulation for migrants in major urban areas such as Milwaukee, and encouraged Mexican Americans to settle into the area.

As Sheboygan's Mexican community grew, so did their efforts to create more inviting spaces in educational and cultural settings. A small group of Mexican Americans formed Amigos Latinos in the late 1960s as one of the first groups in the city focused on creating a cultural space for the growing community. The organization was offered space at St. Clement Church and held its first Fiesta Latina in 1968 in collaboration with students from South High School and the University of Wisconsin–Sheboygan. Amigos Latinos petitioned the pastor to lead Masses in Spanish and gathered funds from the community to purchase a large image of Our Lady of Guadalupe to place in the sanctuary and celebrate her feast day throughout the 1970s. At South High, administrators and counselors worked with Tejano parents to create bilingual programming for the growing population of Spanish-speaking students, turning to federal funding to support bilingual staff and new curricular offerings.

In Appleton, Chicano community members rallied to create La Raza, Incorporated, in the summer of 1971, a nonprofit organization focused on assisting and educating Mexican Americans in the Fox Cities area. Under the direction of Father Prudencio "Pancho" Oyarbide, a Catholic priest originally from the Basque region of Spain, the organization's priorities covered helping seasonal migrants and settled-out Chicanos, crime prevention, police and judicial reform, alcohol rehabilitation, K–12 and postsecondary education, and social welfare. To spread the wide-ranging work of its members, the organization founded a newspaper called *Adelante Raza!* (which roughly translates to "onward, people!"), as well as a Spanish-language radio program staffed by Mexican migrant youth and run through Waupaca-based Radio WDUX called "La Voz de la Raza" (the voice of the people). Within a few years of their establishment, La Raza, Inc., employed state and federal funding to serve more than 3,200 permanent Spanish-speaking residents in Appleton as well as 3,000–5,000 seasonal migrants in the seven-county area that included Outagamie, Winnebago, Portage, Waushara, Green Lake, Waupaca, and Brown Counties.

La Raza, Inc., principally aimed to activate leadership within the Chicano and broader Latino community in Appleton to join in statewide and nationwide activism. The organization sponsored and facilitated leadership training for Mexican American community members at Blessed Sacrament Fathers Seminary in Waupaca in 1972, with representatives from the eight-county area covered by the organization. The sessions were driven by a "leaders as servants" framework, as Catholic priests who'd been active in the Spanish-speaking community reminded the attendees that "un servidor respeta y escucha para darse cuenta de lo que esta pasando" (a servant respects and listens to understand what is occurring). Many of those trained as local leaders went on to support César Chávez and the United Farm Workers' lettuce and grape boycotts, which put pressure on California growers to settle labor disputes with agricultural workers. Throughout the 1970s, Chicano leaders successfully persuaded local groceries in the Fox Cities area to stop selling boycotted lettuce and to display the black thunderbird of the United Farm Workers. They also invited migrant workers from California to Wisconsin to speak about the boycotts, to educate Wisconsin residents about the labor issues involved and the strategy being used. Others joined UMOS to clean up unsanitary and uncertified migrant camps by working with the Waushara Migrant Health Clinic, a set of clinics serving the health needs of migrant workers in Waushara, Marquette, Portage, and Green Lake Counties. La Raza leaders also urged the Wisconsin attorney general to take legal action against growers that persistently violated workers' protections.

The organization expanded its mission to higher education in 1972 by providing material and leadership support to minority students at the nearby University of Wisconsin–Oshkosh who were protesting for more responsive programming. Members helped recruit Chicano students to the campus; find more stable funding for Chicano students, faculty, and invited speakers; and push to establish culturally relevant courses and incorporate books related to Latinos into the campus's libraries. The following year, the organization supported an ultimately unsuccessful proposal before the Board of Regents to make the University of Wisconsin Center–Fox Valley at Menasha the academic and cultural center for Mexican students in the state. The ultimate goal was to provide a space where Mexican American youth could learn about their own culture and history while working toward a university education and degree.

One of La Raza, Inc.'s longstanding contributions to the state's Chicano movement came in 1973, when the organization received funding from the Wisconsin Humanities Council to hold a conference at Lawrence University on the culture, language, and socioeconomic status of Chicanos in Wisconsin. Called "Strangers in Our Homeland," the program sought to expose the social alienation Spanish speakers faced throughout the state. The Midwest-based El Teatro del Barrio, an affiliate of the National Chicano Theater Organization, performed skits while Chicano folk troubadour Jesus "Chuy" Negrete led the crowd in singing *corridos*. Lectures and presentations on migrant worker rights, bilingual and bicultural education, and community organizing were followed by group discussions that prompted vigorous and productive debate. The successful multiday event produced a bilingual report called "Los Nativos" that detailed proposed methods for breaking down discriminatory barriers that kept Chicanos a "society apart" from the broader white community.

🌿🌿

FIGHTING FOR LATINO POWER
IN WISCONSIN POLITICS

With social service organizations tailored to the Spanish-speaking community blossoming throughout Wisconsin by the early 1970s, Chicano and Latino activists next turned to organizing for political power at the local, state, and federal levels through organizations such as La Raza Unida. Springing from activism initiated by organizations such as the Mexican American Youth Organization (MAYO) and individuals including José Ángel Gutierrez and Mario Compean, La Raza Unida was formed as a Chicano political party in Crystal City, Texas, in 1971. Local branches of the organization supported candidates in elections throughout southwestern states, winning a handful of local and county seats. The organization made its way to Wisconsin in the early 1970s as both a local organization in cities such as Appleton and as a statewide network later in the decade.

In 1973, Wisconsin Latino leaders from thirteen counties joined together to create a network through La Raza Unida to advocate for Latino causes at the state and local levels. Activists hoped to coordinate their efforts to fight discrimination in housing, employment, and law enforcement to create more effective statewide political pressure. In August 1975, more than three hundred Jefferson County residents joined the recently established local branch of La Raza Unida, set up in the region as a nonprofit organization (and thus barred from engaging in explicit political activity). Most of the founders of the branch were former migrants who had come to the area more than ten years earlier to work at Muck Farm in Lake Mills. The organization strove to foster cultural self-awareness and pride while at the same time working for better economic and living conditions for the area's Mexican American community. Operating with a $10,000 government grant to assess the county's Mexican American population and its problems, members set as a lofty goal 100 percent employment for the area's Mexican-descent population. The following year, delegates from the fourteen chapters of La Raza Unida Wisconsin, along with representatives from the Organización Hispana Americana, La Casa de Esperanza, and UMOS met with Governor Patrick Lucey to support proposed legislation that would improve the status of migrant workers in the state. The proposed legislation mandated bilingual contracts for migrants entering the state as well as the guarantee of "reasonable access" to toilets and drinking water for workers, and ensured that migrants wouldn't be forced to work more than sixty hours or six days per week, or more than twelve hours per day.

Chicano political activists also made their voices heard on numerous governor's committees created to study the living and working conditions of Latinos across the state. In 1971, accusations of police harassment made by the Latino community prompted newly elected Wisconsin governor Patrick J. Lucey to commission a committee to examine problems within the state's Spanish-speaking communities. After months of surveys, community meetings, and discussion, the committee released a scathing report that detailed the inability of government programs to fulfill the needs of Latino citizens, describing a "citizenry divorced and ignored by their institutions" and "evidence that faith in society and its institutions have been violated." Listing the failures of city and state government as a "lack of communication; lack of planning; lack of coordination and cooperation; inefficient use of existing facilities; and, lack of funds," the committee called for a wholesale reevaluation of the state's efforts to enact meaningful economic and social change for its Spanish-speaking residents.

The long list of issues cited by the committee echoed the findings of previous reports, including rising unemployment, a lack of educational opportunities, insufficient affordable housing hampered by discriminatory code enforcement, pitiful health and welfare assistance, and deteriorating relationships with law enforcement. From their one-on-one conversations with members of the Latino community, committee members surmised that the only thing that Spanish speakers in Wisconsin asked for was "an opportunity to live in harmony and peace with their neighbors in their communities and their state." Proposing that the government had "the responsibility and the obligation to take the lead in carrying out public policy," the committee deemed that political leaders displayed "a lack of will" to enact change for a Latino community that was demanding results. Along with a long list of recommendations for each specific target area of need, the group called for the governor to appoint a special assistant for minority problems in his office, and advocated for the legislature to increase funding for staffing in the Equal Rights Division to police charges of discrimination in hiring and housing. In addition, the report asked social service agencies to respect the cultural and ethnic heritage of the Latino community, who had come to resent assimilationist programming and requirements tied to any form of welfare or state aid.

Despite the 1971 committee's best efforts to delineate areas for change and advocacy, state politicians moved sluggishly to act on its recommendations. Within five years Governor Lucey established yet another committee called the Governor's Council on Spanish Speaking People and charged its members with once again identifying the areas in which state agencies that served Latinos were not providing adequate services and uncovering where additional services were still needed. The council, composed of citizens and legislators, held public hearings in cities throughout Wisconsin and sent questionnaires to each state agency. Not surprisingly, their final report detailed many of the same issues identified by the 1971 commission, as well as conflicts with affirmative action hiring practices and partially implemented bilingual educational programming. The 1976 commission again implored state officials to act more responsively to Wisconsin's quickly growing Latino community.

Partly in response to the efforts of the 1971 and 1976 commissions, as well as continued activism within the state's Spanish-speaking community, Governor Patrick Lucey signed a bilingual and bicultural education bill into law in May 1976. The education program aimed to help thousands of English-language learners through a transitional language curriculum, and required school districts to establish English-teaching programs wherever a reasonable need for such instruction existed. In this case, "reasonable need" meant ten or more limited-English-speaking students in kindergarten to third grade and twenty or more students in fourth to twelfth grade. The law mandated that the state provide 70 percent of program funding for teacher salaries and curricular materials.

Despite the passage of the bilingual education act, many Wisconsin Latinos came to feel that politicians and elected officials merely engaged in what one community leader referred to as a "legislative ritual" to garner votes during election years. Efforts to establish permanent commissions to serve Latinos were constantly defeated in the Legislature, frustrating activists in their efforts to achieve some form of institutional power. Latinos were heartened, however, when acting governor Martin Schreiber appointed Ness Flores, a leader in the Spanish-speaking community, to a county judgeship in Waukesha County in 1978. The son of a Tejano migrant worker who had settled in Wisconsin, Flores successfully ran for election for the seat in 1980, becoming the first Mexican and Latino to ever sit as an elected judge in the state.

UNDOCUMENTED IMMIGRATION IN THE 1980s

Documented and undocumented immigration from Mexico to the United States grew at high rates throughout the late 1970s and early 1980s. Economists and demographers attributed the rise in immigration to a number of factors, including a series of economic crises that stunned Mexico and pushed the country's joblessness rate to over 20 percent. Unable to secure visas for legal immigration to the United States, some in Mexico made the decision to migrate north to find better employment and thus provide for their families back home. The decision to travel north was never an easy one for these immigrants; it involved leaving behind loved ones, homes, entire communities, and a way of life. While states along the border region became receiving sites for a large number of incoming immigrants, many Mexicans made their way to the Midwest, drawn by promises of industrial and agricultural work. Chicago trailed only Los Angeles as the urban area with the largest concentration of undocumented immigrants throughout the period.

Mexican immigration to Wisconsin continued to grow after the 1970s as factories, tanneries, foundries, canners, and meatpackers began to more heavily recruit Mexican natives—through both legal and extralegal means—to fill an expanding number of grueling, low-paying positions.

Immigration and Naturalization Service (INS) officials estimated that Wisconsin's own undocumented population ranged from twelve to fifteen thousand by the end of the decade. How one "became" undocumented in the eyes of federal law could occur in a number of ways. Some Mexican immigrants made the decision to embark on the dangerous journey across the US–Mexico border without legal visas, paying anonymous brokers called "coyotes" who charged hundreds of dollars for the promise of safe passage into this country. More often than not, however, immigrants of any number of nationalities—including those of Mexican origin—who found themselves outside of proper immigration status did so after overstaying a legally approved work or travel visa.

Those who made the decision to come to the United States *sin papeles* (without papers) faced numerous hurdles with drastic implications for themselves and often the lives of their family members in Mexico. Living in cities like Milwaukee without legal documentation often meant creating a life in the shadows, constantly living in fear: fear of deportation and the economic hardship that might befall their families if they lost their employment; fear of employers who abused their knowledge of workers' immigration status and used it as a tool to dismiss surplus laborers and disrupt worker organization; and fear of a general American public that often considered undocumented immigrants at a minimum unwelcome guests and at worst "illegals" who posed a risk to local and national security. This fear permeated all aspects of life and work for those who lived in the margins. A Mexican father who came with his family to the United States explained to the *Milwaukee Journal*, "You are lonely and afraid because you are not in your own country. You feel angry, but there is nothing you can do. There is nowhere to run."

Undocumented immigrants' feelings of dread and anxiety were often exacerbated by increased federal immigration raids at worksites in southeast Wisconsin in the early 1980s. Latino community leaders expressed anger that undocumented immigrants of Latin American descent were targeted in massive federal raids, while those from European countries— especially those who hailed from regions under Communist rule that were deemed of higher importance for national security—were treated with a larger degree of leniency. Wisconsin Latinos were especially affronted when INS officials initiated a series of deportation raids throughout the state during National Hispanic Heritage Week in 1983. These actions prompted Mexican American leaders to contact Governor Tony Earl to demand that he intervene against roundups that were "worse than a slap in the face" to the community.

Latinos in Wisconsin publicly decried these ongoing raids as unmerited and discriminatory, and rejected claims that undocumented immigrants were a drain on American society or that they were stealing jobs from American citizens. Study after study showed that undocumented workers worked longer hours for less pay than American citizens in comparable jobs, while paying more in taxes and wage deductions than they received in social services. Many employers bypassed federal minimum wage laws by paying undocumented workers outside of the US tax system. One undocumented farm laborer working in the state explained to a *Milwaukee Journal* reporter, "It's not much money and it's hard work. People in this country don't work [for] that type of money. People here work eight hours and that's it. If it wasn't for us, the man's vegetables would spoil and rot. That's the truth." Another worker, employed sorting metals, understood that his lack of English skills and documentation status served as barriers to promotion: "I can't defend myself or fight back, so I just work in silence. But I can see that I'll be doing the same job as long as I remain here."

Rising rates of immigration and reports of employer abuses against undocumented workers led federal legislators to debate the breadth and inclusivity of immigration reform throughout the early 1980s. In 1986, Congress passed the Immigration Reform and Control Act, signed into law by President Ronald Reagan. This major revision of federal law sought to curb undocumented immigration by increasing border security and strengthening employer sanctions for knowingly hiring undocumented workers. But it also created a pathway to legalized status for people already living in the country without documentation. The legalization provision allowed undocumented immigrants who had lived in the United States since before January 1, 1982, to receive temporary resident status and eventually work toward citizenship. Nationwide, approximately four million undocumented immigrants applied for legalization through the newly created pathway before the decade's end.

In Wisconsin, social service and religious organizations such as Catholic Social Services, the International Institute, and La Casa de Esperanza set up aid centers to help undocumented people apply for legal status. Staff and volunteers counseled immigrants on the preregistration process and helped them fill out the necessary paperwork. These organizations also served as buffers between the undocumented community and INS officials, as many immigrants remained wary of interacting with agents of the federal government after the deportation raids of the early 1980s. Fears within the undocumented community of continued government surveillance and possible deportation prevented many from applying for legalization. While officials estimated that more than twelve thousand people could be eligible for relief, fewer than a third actually applied through the federal government. Yolanda Ayubi, a project coordinator at the Social Development Commission and a member of the Milwaukee Hispanic Coalition, explained, "There is a deep fear. It's hard for a person who has always been hiding his tracks—using another name or social security number—to go and uncover everything that's been covered."

While popular media coverage focused on the uptick in undocumented immigration throughout the period, the majority of growth within Wisconsin's Mexican-descent community in fact came from its American-born population. According to the 1980 census, Wisconsin's Latino population had grown to sixty-three thousand people, or about 1.3 percent of the state, 65 percent of which claimed Mexican descent. Three-quarters of Wisconsinites were born in the United States, while more than 80 percent of Mexicans were born stateside. This population was comparatively younger than the general population; while 33 percent of the state's population was under twenty years old, that number grew to more than 50 percent within the Mexican community. In Milwaukee—a city that trailed only Chicago and Detroit in the Midwest with regard to Latino population—a 1983 survey conducted by the *Milwaukee Journal* found that more Latinos living in the city had grown up in the metro area than in Mexico. A third of all Latinos interviewed were in fact native Wisconsinites, while many had moved to Wisconsin as children. These Mexican Americans who had lived their whole—or close to their whole—lives as Americans were more likely than their forebears to be bilingual and educated, having benefited from the reforms that gave them improved access to the public school system and university educations. While still facing discrimination in schools and workplaces, many were able to find work in a variety of professions, from entrepreneurs to educators, positioning them to be better advocates for newer immigrants.

EMERGENT POLITICAL AND BUSINESS POWER

As the national Latino population continued to grow, political scientists commented that more and more eligible Latino voters would help make the 1980s the "decade of the Hispanics." While some Latinos did rise to elected positions in parts of the country with more concentrated Spanish-speaking populations, Latinos in Wisconsin struggled to transform the activism of the previous decades into victories at the polls. Manuel Salas, serving as one of a handful of Wisconsin Latino delegates to the 1984 Democratic National Convention, argued that political change could occur through protests as well as through party politics. Activists could point to a handful of victories, including the passage of the Bilingual Education Act, the Migrant Education Bill, and the waiver of residency requirements for migrant students, but many found the progress too slow and gradual. The inception of various governors' committees to investigate the economic conditions of Spanish speakers in the state in the 1970s had in part led to the appointment of some Latinos to advisory positions on legislative and executive task forces. But many in Latino communities in Wisconsin felt silenced without elected representatives who explicitly listened to their demands. Filberto Murguia, director of the Council for the Spanish Speaking, implored elected officials to take Latinos' interests seriously. He told the *Milwaukee Journal,* "We're not asking for favors and we don't want handouts. . . . We want to help people so they can help themselves."

As they had done decades earlier, Latinos continued to build coalitions to better assert their rights to educational reform across the state. Latino professionals in higher education formed the Wisconsin Hispanic Council on Higher Education in 1983 under the direction of council president Andrea "Tess" Arenas, who at the time was serving as assistant director of La Casa de Esperanza. Among other goals, the council sought to push legislators to act more responsively to the Latino community's educational needs. The organization, based at the University of Wisconsin–Whitewater, consisted of thirty-five Latinos in positions in the University of Wisconsin System, private colleges, and the private sector. Members conducted research on Latino dropout rates at the high school level and studied Latino access to and enrollment in the state's higher education system. While their research aimed to inform legislators and business leaders on how to create better entry points for minority students in higher education, the members also served as visible role models for first-generation Latino college students across the state.

Wisconsin's Latino political clout also grew gradually throughout the late 1980s and 1990s. In 1986, Governor Tony Earl appointed Ness Flores, a former Tejano migrant worker, Waukesha County circuit judge, and chairman of the State Public Service Commission, to the University of Wisconsin Board of Regents. Nearly two decades later Governor Jim Doyle appointed Jesus Salas, the firebrand migrant union organizer who had once stormed the halls of the Wisconsin State Assembly, to the same position. Throughout the late 1980s and 1990s, voters elected more people of Mexican descent to positions around the state. In Madison, Rosa Escamilla served as an alder on the city's Common Council, and Juan José Lopez served as president of the Madison School Board. In Waukesha Richard Hernandez served on the Common Council and ran unsuccessfully for mayor and a state Assembly seat. Latinos of other national descent also served in elected positions. Puerto Rican Pedro Colón became the first Latino state representative in 1998, while Cuban-descent Elsa Lamelas was appointed and then reelected as a circuit judge in 1993. In 2010, JoCasta Zamarripa became the first person of Mexican descent to be elected to the Wisconsin State Assembly, representing the predominately Latino Eighth Assembly District that Colón had previously served.

Latino business leaders also worked to foster economic development in Spanish-speaking communities throughout Wisconsin. Founded as the Latin American Chamber of Commerce in 1969 before incorporating and rebranding itself in 1972, the Milwaukee Hispanic Chamber of Commerce encouraged entrepreneurship and business initiatives among Latinos throughout southeast Wisconsin. The Chamber also sponsored Mexican Independence Day festivities throughout the 1970s and early 1980s, which often included parades, carnivals, beauty contests, and dances held on the city's south side. In 1989, María Monreal Cameron became the organization's director and one of the only Latina leaders of a social or business organization in the state. Cameron's business acumen stretched back into her family's history. The Monreales had first come to Milwaukee from Texas in the 1940s and were known for their El Matador restaurants. In her new position, Cameron identified a rising entrepreneurial passion among the city's Latinos, stating, "There's smoke there. We just have to stir up the ashes to build a fire." As director she worked to challenge a troublesome sense of sexism and prejudice in the area's business scene, all the while diversifying the Chamber's board by encouraging Latina leadership in business and social avenues throughout the community. Always focused on expanding educational opportunities for the city's young Latino community, the Chamber established the Hispanic Chamber of Commerce of Wisconsin/Phillip Arreola Scholarship Program in 1993 for Latino high school seniors making their way into higher education.

GROWING COMMUNITIES, GROWING PAINS

Despite federal legislators' efforts to curb documented and undocumented immigration flows from Latin American countries in the 1980s, migration to the United States from Mexico continued at a record pace through the 1990s. Economists have attributed the rapid uptick in these immigration patterns to international trade pacts such as the North American Free Trade Agreement (NAFTA). Despite being acclaimed as a boon for corporations and regional trade, the agreement had the unintended consequence of devastating Mexico's agricultural industry. With declining wages and fewer economic opportunities throughout Mexico, many farmers and residents of rural communities made the decision to migrate to the United States throughout the decade. Mexican immigrants arrived in towns and cities across Wisconsin in search of better economic opportunities, many times venturing to locations previously unexplored by past Spanish-speaking pioneers. In 1990, more than 93,000 people of Latino heritage called the state home, and by the end of the decade, that number had risen to more than 193,000.

While Milwaukee County continued to be home to the state's largest Mexican and Latino populations throughout the end of the century, new arrivals helped spur the development of Mexican communities in cities and towns across Wisconsin. Throughout the 1980s, Waukesha's Latino community continued to be one of the fastest-growing segments of the city's population, comprising 5 percent of the area's community. Concentrated on the city's east side near the Strand, the original point of arrival for many Mexicanos who came to Waukesha in the early twentieth century, Latinos continued to advocate for expanded budgets for schools and social services. Walter Sava, executive director of La Casa de Esperanza, Inc., the primary social service agency for Latinos in Waukesha, helped lead efforts to improve the city's bilingual education programming as well as improve vocational training and job counseling services throughout the late twentieth century. By the 2000s, nearly fifteen thousand Latino residents lived in the Waukesha area, accounting for 10 percent of the city's population.

Latino communities have continued to grow in cities and towns around Wisconsin, both in areas that have a rich history of Spanish-speaking settlement and in newer regions as well. In southeastern counties like Racine and Kenosha, Latinos—many of them now third- or fourth-generation Mexican Americans—have joined a statewide trend in being one of the fastest-growing demographic groups in the state. Between 2000 and 2009, Washington County's Latino population increased by 76 percent to 2,693, while Ozaukee County saw an increase of 58 percent to 1,699. The 2010 US Census tallied more than two thousand Latinos living in La Crosse and the surrounding area, an increase of 10 percent over the previous ten years. Multiethnic efforts responding to this growth helped establish the Centro Latino in 2014 at the First Baptist Church as a joint effort between Viterbo University, the immigration task force of an interfaith social justice group, Catholic Charities, the Franciscan Sisters of Perpetual Adoration, and the University of Wisconsin–La Crosse. Like many other social service community organizations around the state, Centro works not only to provide social and legal services to Latinos but also to educate the broader La Crosse community about Latino immigration and culture.

Between 1990 and 2000, Dane County's Latino population grew 150 percent, and by 2015 Latinos accounted for 6.3 percent of the county's population. Within its Spanish-speaking community, Dane County continues to display the broadest multinational diversity in the state as Mexicans account for only 60 percent of the Latino population. Madison's largest Latino-serving organization, Centro Hispano, opened in February 1983 thanks to funding aid provided by the United Way of Dane County. Initially created to meet the needs of a large community of incoming Cuban refugees settled in Dane County, Centro also serves the permanent community of more than three thousand Latinos in Madison with representatives from nearly every Latin American country. Centro's primary goal was to create English courses in coordination with the Madison Literacy Center and OMEGA School, a general equivalency diploma center. That mission has expanded to referral services for non–English speakers to build bridges between the Spanish-speaking and the general Madison community.

In Green Bay, Mexican and Mexican American migration to the city remained small through the mid-1970s. Some laborers and their families came to Green Bay as recruits to work in the city's meatpacking industry, but the community could count fewer than fifty members by the late 1970s. It was not until between 1980 and 2000 that Green Bay and Brown County saw a large increase in their Mexican-descent population, due in large part to a growing meatpacking industry in the area. Louis Sánchez, who left behind his small Mexican village to find work at the Packerland Packing Company in the 1980s, told a researcher, "People come to a better life. They take their chances, and as soon as they come to Green Bay they are regular working families." Between 1990 and 2000, the city's Latino population increased sevenfold. By the end of the twentieth century, Brown County had become home to the third-largest Latino community in the state. At Saint Willebrord Catholic Parish, Father Ken De Grot, Father Harvey Toonen, and Sister Melanie Maczka were instrumental in outreach to arriving Mexicans and other Spanish speakers throughout the 1980s and 1990s, helping establish celebrations such as Our Lady of Guadalupe and Las Posadas in Spanish.

A resurging meatpacking industry continued to drive Mexican immigration to Green Bay through the 1990s, spurring the establishment of Latino-owned businesses catering to the growing community and more Spanish-speaking students in Brown County schools. The 2000 census showed that Green Bay's Latino population had grown from one thousand in 1990 to more than seven thousand, and by 2008, estimates placed that number closer to fifteen thousand. The rapid growth of the Latino community created a sense of culture shock for a city that had been for generations much more homogenous, and led to a series of divisive debates at the local legislative level. In response to the growing number of Spanish speakers in the area, the Brown County Board passed an ordinance declaring English the official language of the county in 2002. The Green Bay Common Council followed that action by adopting legislation allowing the city to revoke the license of any business that employed undocumented immigrants. In passing the employer bill, the council president declared, "It's a message to the illegal alien community that says you are not welcome. Don't come here." Both laws drew opposition from Green Bay's Latino organizations, the bishop of the Catholic Archdiocese, the American Civil Liberties Union, and the national Mexican American Legal Defense Fund. Among newcomers from Latin America and those who had lived in the area for years, the laws had the chilling effect of sending a message to all Latinos: regardless of their citizenship status, they were not welcome in the county.

LOOKING TO THE FUTURE

On February 18, 2016, more than twenty thousand people—immigrants, native-born sons and daughters, and their allies—took to the streets around the state's capitol building and marched inside of it to protest anti-immigrant legislation and a growing sense of anti-Latino ardor that seemed to be catching hold across the United States. Organized by immigrants' rights organizations such as the Milwaukee-based Voces de la Frontera, the protesters gathered in opposition to two separate bills under consideration by legislators. Assembly Bill 450 proposed to force local police officers to question any person suspected of having committed a crime about his or her immigration status and detain them for deportation if there were discrepancies in their status, while Senate Bill 369 aimed to block counties statewide from issuing local identification cards to people who couldn't access state versions.

The proposed legislation in Wisconsin arrived amidst renewed national conversations around Mexican immigration to the United States. The presidential election of 2016 witnessed yet another national upsurge in anti-immigrant fervor, this time spurred on by unfounded statements made by the Republican candidate Donald Trump. While he may not have known it at the time, when the soon-to-be-elected president accused the Mexican government of sending "rapists," drug dealers, and other criminals to the United States, he was in fact drawing on well-worn narratives of criminality that have stretched back a century. These allegations based on racist stereotypes, coupled with promises of a new wall to be constructed along the United States–Mexico border, placed immigrants again in the center of conversations around criminality, employment, citizenship, and national belonging. Across the nation, people of Mexican descent found themselves newly vilified and made part of a new "Mexican problem," with their legal standing and their very right to exist in this country called into question.

Those who gathered at the state capitol in February thus organized to confront both immediate attacks on their legal and civil rights in their communities as well as national efforts to disparage an entire immigrant and immigrant-descent community. The protests served as a call to arms, as thousands of workers walked off their jobs on a one-day strike to demonstrate their vitality and importance to the state's economy. Chanting "el pueblo unido jámas será vencido," translated to "the people united will never be defeated," immigrants and their allies successfully pushed back legislation that would have empowered local police officers to surveil, detain, and help deport those without legal documentation in the state's towns and cities. The collective action of these protesters helped to defeat AB 450, while bringing to light the growing power of Wisconsin's Latino community.

In the wake of the protests, many Wisconsinites were surprised to learn that the state had such a large and vibrant Latino population. While they may have been mistaken in the idea that this community was a new occurrence, they would have been correct in assessing the recently rapid growth in the size of the state's Latino people. According to demographic reports, Latinos' share in the state's overall population has grown from 2 percent in 1990 to 3.5 percent in 2000 to 6.3 percent in 2013. However, Wisconsin's Latino population, and specifically its varied Mexican-descent communities, have a history in this state that reaches back more than a century.

As they grow in number, Mexican American voices have made themselves heard in a variety of ways in Wisconsin. Dane County has recently welcomed the state's second Latino writer as a citywide poet laureate. Oscar Mireles was selected to serve as Madison's poet laureate from 2016 to 2018. Born in Racine to a migrant farmworker mother and factory worker father, Mireles has been a community leader and educator in southeast Wisconsin for decades. Besides his role as director of the alternative education school Omega in Madison, Mireles is also the editor of *I Didn't Know There Were Latinos in Wisconsin*, a bilingual anthology of poetry, memoir, and fiction from Wisconsin Latino writers. Mireles followed in the footsteps of Brenda Cárdenas, who previously had served as the poet laureate of Milwaukee from 2010 to 2012. Cárdenas, a Milwaukee native and associate professor of English at the University of Wisconsin–Milwaukee, is the author of numerous bilingual anthologies of poetry. Her appointment to the position represented the culmination of a nearly one-hundred-year-old history of the Milwaukee Mexican story: her paternal grandfather came to the city from Mexico in the 1920s as one of *los primeros* to work in tanneries and foundries, and her grandparents José and Mercedes opened Cárdenas Grocery on the city's near south side in the 1940s.

Mexican Americans have made wide-ranging cultural contributions in Wisconsin—from influential Mexican writers, muralists, and musicians to popular Mexican eateries—but perhaps no event celebrating Mexican and Latino culture is better known than Milwaukee's Mexican Fiesta, held every late August at the city's Summerfest grounds. The three-day gathering traces its roots back to the late 1960s, when Summerfest organizers first included aspects of Mexican culture into the citywide festival with performances by the Flying Indians of Acapulco (an indigenous folk group re-creating Aztec rituals) and the National Ballet of Mexico. In 1978, the Latin American Union for Civil Rights (LAUCR) began its own Mexican Independence Day festival in mid-September called Fiesta Mexicana, a two-day celebration held at the Summerfest grounds with sponsorship from the Miller Brewing Company. The early iterations of the festival began with a Mass conducted in Spanish, after which attendees enjoyed the musical stylings of popular acts that played mariachi, conjunto, ranchera, and salsa music. The festival also featured traditional dances and booths serving Mexican cuisine.

In the early 1980s, organizers moved Fiesta to the warmth of late August and expanded the celebration into a three-day event concluding Summerfest's slate of ethnic festivals. Throughout its tenure, the festivities have emphasized bringing world-class Latin American entertainment to Milwaukee at a reasonable price for fairgoers. Organizers coordinated with the Mexican Department of Tourism to feature traditional folk performers like La Guelaguetza de Oaxaca, a dancing troupe representing the seven tribes of the Mexican state of Oaxaca, as well as the secretary of tourism of the state of Veracruz to bring the dynamic Jarochos de Veracruz to Wisconsin. The event has grown to include jalapeño-eating and tortilla-making contests; a competition for the best Mexican *grito*, or holler; a market with local and international vendors selling handmade

imported pottery and jewelry; and historical photographic exhibits documenting Milwaukee's early Mexican community. In the late 1980s the
Wisconsin Hispanic Scholarship Foundation assumed control of the festival and helped expand the fund-raising efforts to provide scholarships
for higher education for Latino students. Today, Mexican Fiesta wel-
comes tens of thousands of visitors to the Summerfest grounds every year
for music, merriment, and plenty of delicious food.

Cultural events such as Mexican Fiesta have been but one prominent
illustration of the gradual incorporation of Mexican communities into
the state. The rapid expansion of bilingual education across Wisconsin
school districts over the last decade indicates a growing appreciation for
multiculturalism as well as Spanish language learning. As in the past,
many of these initiatives have arisen from community concerns regarding educational equity. In Madison, for example, community members
and educators came together to found Nuestro Mundo Community Elementary School in the early 2000s to serve the rapidly growing Latino
population and address opportunity gaps for Spanish-speaking students.
The dual-language immersion school follows an innovative classroom
model incorporating half Spanish- and half English-dominant students
learning both languages through academic content. When it graduated
its first high school class of fully bilingual students in 2017, among the
proud parents and educators cheering on the graduates was Luz
Celedón, a Nuestro Mundo teacher and proud daughter of a migrant
worker family. Known throughout the city's Latino community for her
passion and advocacy, Luz was named the 2014 Bilingual Educator of the
Year by the Wisconsin Association for Bilingual Education in recognition
of her dedication to her students and their families.

These examples of celebration and education have only just begun
the long road toward acceptance of not only Mexican culture but more
importantly people of Mexican descent as integral and valued members
of Wisconsin's broader community. The proposed 2016 Wisconsin legislation and the racist rhetoric espoused by political leaders across the
nation echo sentiments that had driven previous calls for immigrant
quotas and deportation raids that have plagued Wisconsin's Mexican
community since it first began a hundred years ago. As they did in the
1920s and the 1980s, the challenges to the legitimacy of Mexican immigration and settlement in the state are driven today by many of the same
fears of the past: fear of the other or the different, fear of change, and

fear of the loss of economic opportunities. But just as previous attempts to curtail national and local population changes were unsuccessful, current efforts to stymie the broadening of the state's community seem also to be bearing little fruit.

In spite of efforts to curtail immigration from Latin American countries such as Mexico, census and demographic reports bear out a very different future for the state. The number of minorities living in Wisconsin will nearly triple over the next half century, according to demographic analysis. No population in the state will grow larger or faster than Latinos, who are projected to go from more than 336,000 Wisconsin residents in 2010 to nearly 1 million by 2060. Among those of Latin American descent living in the state, 70 percent report being of Mexican heritage. In Milwaukee County, which continues to have the state's largest concentration of Latino population, Latinos have come to account for nearly all of the city's net demographic growth since 1990 and have been crucial to the area's economic vitality and survival. The histories of those who came before, such as *los primeros*, the pioneer Mexicans who created their homes in Milwaukee in the 1920s, demonstrate that a spirit of perseverance in the face of hardship and adversity will continue to guide future immigrants and settlers as they fight to *seguir adelante*.

🌿

ORAL HISTORY OF GRACIELA DE LA CRUZ

Born in Nuevo Laredo, Tamaulipas, Graciela De La Cruz moved to the United States at the age of nine with her parents and eleven brothers and sisters in 1950, when her father secured stable employment in Texas. Pursuing better work, the family eventually settled in Milwaukee in 1953. While her parents encouraged her to do well in primary and secondary school, her father forbade her from pursuing a college education because he was afraid it might lead to Graciela losing her Mexican cultural identity. Graciela met her future husband, Luis, at a cultural celebration at the International Institute in the 1950s. They would go on to be significant supporters of Mexican folk music and dancing in Milwaukee through the end of the twentieth century. Below, Graciela describes how she was finally able to attend college in the late 1960s and how that experience kindled a passion for community activism. This excerpt is from an interview with the author on January 10, 2017.

I always used to say, "I'm going to go to the university, I'm going to go to the university," but at that point I had two children. One day I received a call from the Spanish Center, also known as the Council for the Spanish Speaking. That's where everything changed, in 1968. I had just had my second daughter, and she was barely three months old. I told my husband Luis, "I have to work at night," because we weren't earning enough. They gave me work from six to nine o'clock at night, where I first started as a receptionist. I would then substitute for the adult basic education classes, without any experience but just a short training. They eventually gave me a class of thirty students! The classes were of older, respectful men and women, many from Cuba, Puerto Rico, and Mexico, and even a student from Russia. I began to teach, earning $2.50. It wasn't a lot, but it helped.

While I was teaching, a young man from Washington, DC, representing the Great Society programs, came to observe our classes. I explained to him that I wasn't a teacher, but he asked to observe my class anyway. He sat in the back of my class, writing and writing. He then asked me, "How much college do you have?" I told him, "None, but I was very good in school and was even in honor society." He then gave me his card and told me to go to Alverno College, to go see a specific counselor, and to tell them that he had sent me.

I went to Alverno, and I took a set of exams. They told me, "You'd be great, but we can't offer you a scholarship because you're married and have children. You're welcome to enroll, but we can't help with financial aid." The counselor recommended I go to the University of Wisconsin–Milwaukee, where they were starting a special program for Latinos and African Americans. And I said, "Well, I'll go!" At UW–M, they looked at my grades and said, "You're in. We need women, and we need Hispanics."

At that point, I thought, "Oh, boy, now I have to talk to Luis." I thought about how I would tell him the news, and I knew I needed to be smart about it. I explained to him, "Look, Luis, I'm not going to go to school for very long. I'm just going to go for one semester, because maybe I'm too old to be doing this." Yeah right, just one semester . . . after I got my bachelor's degree, I got a master's degree, and then a second master's degree! Well, he agreed that I should go to school, and once I got started, I knew that I needed, and would keep going. The only thing that I asked Luis was that he buy me a dryer to help with washing and drying our children's diapers.

With the taking care of the home and children, it was difficult, but my students loved me. They would say to me, "You're going to become a teacher, you have to become a teacher." I would have been one of the only certified teachers at the Spanish Center, where I kept working while I attended university.

Luis helped me so much, of that there is no doubt. He would drive me to the Spanish Center because we only had one car—we lived on the northwest side and the center was on the south side—and then he would pick me up at the end of the night with our daughters in pajamas, and then he would bathe them and put them to bed and everything, giving me time to study until one o'clock in the morning. And then I would wake up the next morning and start all over again. I lost a lot of weight during that time, that's for sure! It was hard, but we did it.

Beyond that, I was an activist. While I was a student, we took over the university in 1970. The activist group was made up of people from Puerto Rico and Texas, and I was one of the people from the local Latino community, and we fought for a just cause. I was afraid that the university would do something to me for being a part of the protests. I told CELA [Committee for the Education of Latin Americans] that if there were going to be problems with the police and if people were going to jail, I wouldn't do it because my daughters needed me. And Luis supported me when I was an activist as well. All the while, I still had to take care of my studies. I would go and march with the activists, but I never missed a class.

We were fighting for an outreach program. Chancellor [J. Martin] Klotsche had told [Jesus] Salas and [Ernesto] Chacón that he would start a program, but he never followed through. They got tired of waiting, and waiting, and waiting. I became a militant . . . well, I already was one, but anyways [laughs]. Remember, I was still at the Spanish Center. And whenever there were meetings with [Father James] Groppi and that whole group, I was always there listening in. I would be teaching, but whenever I had ten minutes of break, I would go over to their meetings to see what was going on. Thus, indirectly, I knew what they were planning for. And then they decided, "We're going to yell, and we're going to sing, and we're going to take over." I told them that I would join along in all the actions, except for missing my classes or going to jail. We had a protest, and five people were arrested. Because of our protest and sit-ins, they established the outreach institute. That was the beginning of my activism, but certainly not the end.

LOST AND FOUND LANGUAGE, OSCAR MIRELES

Oscar Mireles was named the fifth poet laureate of Madison—and the first Latino poet to hold that distinction—in December 2015, to serve from 2016 to 2018. Mireles grew up in Racine, Wisconsin, as one of eleven children of a migrant farmworker mother and factory worker father. For more than thirty-five years, he has composed poetry on various aspects of the Latino experience and has had his work featured in more than fifty publications. He has also edited three volumes of work by Wisconsin-based Latino writers for his series I Didn't Know There Were Latinos in Wisconsin *and is a renowned educator as executive director of the alternative Omega School in Madison. The poem below reflects on the pressure on Latino immigrants to assimilate and the difficulty of being an activist who did not grow up bilingual. More of Mireles's work can be found on his website, www.oscarmireles.com.*

It started in 1949, when my oldest brother
came home from school
in Racine, Wisconsin
after flunking kindergarten
because he 'spoke no English'
and declared to my parents
that 'the rest of the kids have to learn to speak English
if we planned on staying here in the United States.'

so my parents lined up
the rest of the seven younger children
had us straighten up
tilt our heads back
reached in our mouth with their hands
and took turns
slicing our tongues in half

making a simple, but unspoken contract
that from then on
the parents would speak Spanish
and the children would respond
back only in English

how do you lose a native language?
does it get misplaced
in the recesses of your brain?
or does it never quite stick to the sides
of your mind?

for me it would always start
with the question
from a brown faced stranger
'hables espanol?'
which means
'do you speak Spanish?'

which meant
if they had to ask me
if I spoke Spanish
this was not going to be a good start for
at having a conversation . . .

my face would start to get flushed
with redness and before
I had a chance to stammer the words 'I don't'

I could see it in their eyes
looking at my embarrassed face
searching for an answer
that they already knew

as I walked away
I know they were thinking
'Who is this guy?'
'How can he not speak his mother's tongue?'
'Where did he grow up anyways?'
'Doesn't he have any pride in knowing who he is?' or
    'Where he came from?'

I tried to reply,
but as the words in Spanish

floated down from my brain
they caught in my teeth,
the rocks of shame.
I spoke in half-tongue.

my future wife
taught me how
to speak Spanish
mainly
by being Colombian
and not speaking English

and I had already known
the language of hands and love
which got me confident enough
to reach deep inside
myself
to find the beautiful sounds and Latin rhythms
that laid deep within me

and although
I still feel my heart jump a beat
when someone asks 'hables espanol?'
now the Spanish resonates within me
and echos back 'si, y usted tambien?'

and today as I talk with the Spanish speaking students
in our school
they can not only feel my words
they can feel my warm heart
splash ancient Spanish sounds off
my native tongue
that has finally grown whole again.

ACKNOWLEDGMENTS

This book is filled with the voices of the millions of people of Mexican descent who have come to Wisconsin to make the state their home, either temporarily or permanently. Because of the scarcity of preserved archival materials documenting Wisconsin's Mexican history, oral histories have been vital for capturing the daily lived experiences of these sojourners. I have been fortunate to meet many people across the state who have been ready and willing to share their stories. I would like to specifically thank those who have taken the time to sit down and have their chronicles recorded: Jesus Salas, Joseph Cárdenas and Elita Cárdenas Kotnik, Ray Bacalzo, Graciela and Luis De La Cruz, Elvira Sándoval-Denk, Guadalupe Macias, the Gonzales family, the Rios family, Oscar Mireles, Jesse Garza, Roberto Rivera, Dr. Tony Báez, Francisco Urbina, and Dr. Enrique Figueroa. Their voices enrich and enliven the narrative of this book.

My own dedication to Wisconsin's Latino history follows in the footsteps of Arnoldo Sevilla and Margarita Sandoval Skare, tireless public historians who have worked diligently over several decades to preserve our community's history. I would also like to thank Dr. Andrea "Tess" Arenas, who set the example of engaged community scholarship through her important work compiling the oral histories of Wisconsin's Latina activists, and whose commitment to her community served as a model for my own work. The invaluable mentorship of these three has nurtured my interest and passion for our state's Latino history.

I would like to thank all three of my advisors during my time at the University of Wisconsin–Madison—the late Camille Guérin-Gonzales, William Jones, and Cindy I-Fen Cheng—who have encouraged me to pursue the academic endeavors that I hold most dear to my heart. I am especially grateful to Will for opening doors at the Wisconsin Historical Society Press, and for encouraging me to take on the work of writing a whole book while trying to finish a dissertation.

The work of any historian is made infinitely easier with the support of dedicated archivists and librarians, and I count myself lucky to have had knowledgeable guides throughout the writing of this book. Thank you to archivists at the Wisconsin and Milwaukee County Historical

Societies, the Milwaukee Public Library, and the Archives Catholic Archdiocese of Milwaukee, all masters of their realms who open doors for re-
searchers such as myself every day.

Taking this book from a proposal to a finished product was ultimately
a collaborative effort. I greatly appreciate the entire team at the Wisconsin Historical Society Press, and especially my editor Erika Wittekind,
who helped me craft a narrative that is hopefully engaging and accessi-
ble for all Wisconsinites, and Jere Foley, for his work to turn this manu-
script into a book.

The stories of my family are infused in every page that I've written,
as their stories are the stories of this community. My own migration story
begins with my grandparents, Papá Javier and Mamá Sipriana (Pana)
Martin and Papá Pedro and Mamá Avelina González, who made innu-
merable sacrifices to come to this country so their families could have a
better life. My parents, Sergio Armando and Bertha, have likewise la-
bored and overcome seemingly insurmountable barriers so that my
brother Alejandro and I could reach summits they might never have
imagined. I am forever indebted to my wonderful wife, Laura, who has
graciously read draft upon draft of so much of my work and continues
to encourage my academic and activist interests. The newest and most
welcome additions to my family, her parents, have also been ready and
willing listeners to these stories; I'd especially like to thank my mother-in-
law Carol Troyer-Shank, who donated her labor by transcribing many of
the oral histories that form the foundation of this book. I love you all
dearly.

Finally, I'd like to extend my deepest gratitude to the countless activists who have fought to make Wisconsin a more welcoming space for
people of all ethnic and racial backgrounds, and especially for those who
have advocated tirelessly for people of Mexican and Latino descent. This
story is ultimately yours, and I only hope that we can continue to add
more chapters to it as we continue the fight. ¡La lucha sigue adelante!

ABOUT THE AUTHOR

Sergio M. González is a doctoral candidate in the University of Wisconsin–Madison Department of History with research interests in American labor, immigration, and working class history. His research investigates Milwaukee's Latino community throughout the twentieth century, focusing on the role of religion in creating interethnic and intraethnic communities, organizations, and social justice movements.

INDEX TO COME

Schmitt, Henry, 33
Schön, Maria Catherine, 6–7
Schramek, Robert, 69
Schreiber, Martin, 113
Scotti, Alfredo, 40
Sevilla, Carlos, 79
Sevilla Chávez, Miguel, 17, 18
Shaw, Barry, 67
Sheboygan, WI, 107–108
Smith, Bill, 65–66
Smith, Ken, 74
social life, 16–19, 27, 29, 33, 39, 75, 76, 79, 107, 118
social services. *See* public welfare
Spanish Baptist Church (Milwaukee), 74
Spanish Center, 77–79, 87, 127–129
Spanish language, 20, 22–23, 28, 31, 38, 39, 51, 56, 73, 81, 85, 86, 87, 103, 107, 130–132
  newspapers, 17, 30–31, 70, 84–85, *92*, *93*, 108
  radio programs, 31–32, 108
  See also education
Spanish Speaking Outreach Institute, 96, 98–99, 129
sports, 12, 23–24, 28, 34, 40, 55, 75, 76
Spring Lake, WI, 63
strikes, 14–15, 69–70, 92, 123
Sturgeon Bay, WI, 51, 62
Sturtevant, WI, 72
surveys. *See under* research

tanneries, 8, 12, 14–15, 24, 31, 36, 107, 113, 124
Tejanos, 49–56, 60-61, 63, 65–71, 74, *89*, *91*, 107, 127–129
Thomson, Vernon W., 35–36
Thunderbirds, 74–75
Tijerina, Felix, 36
Toonen, Harvey, 121
Torres, John, 85
Torres, Mauro, 32
Torres, Miguelo, 34
Tovar, Catherine, 40
Truman, Harry, 53
Trump, Donald, 122

unemployment, 24, 80, 86, 102, 111
Unión Beneficia Hispana, 85–86
Union Grove, WI, 25
United Community Center, 74–76
United Electrical, Radio, and Machine Workers, 83
United Farm Workers, 67, 71, 100, 109
United Migrant Opportunity Services, Incorporated (UMOS), 72–73, 87, 102, 103, 106, 107, 109, 111
United States
  Commission on Civil Rights, 85, 87
  Office of Economic Opportunity, 77, 79
  Office of Immigration and Naturalization, 25, 57, 114–115, 116
  Presidential Commission on Migrant Labor, 53
  Senate Subcommittee on Migratory Labor, 54
University of Wisconsin–Fox Valley, 109
University of Wisconsin–Madison, 100, 106
University of Wisconsin–Milwaukee, 10, 28, *96*, 98–99, 100, 124, 128–129
University of Wisconsin–Oshkosh, 99–100, 109
University of Wisconsin–Superior, 101
University of Wisconsin–Whitewater, 100–101, 117
Uribe, Antonio C., 27
Uribe, Ted, 86
Usabel, Salvadore, 106

Valdes, David, Jr., 27, 28
Valdes, David, Sr., 29
Valdes, Gilberto, 36
Valdes, Loreto, 32
Valdez, Avelardo "Lalo," 84
Valdovinos, Gladys, 35
Valdovinos, Salvador, 28–29, 35
Villa, Francisco "Pancho," 9, 12
Viva Jalisco, 27, 32
Voces de la Frontera, 122
Voz Mexicana, La (newspaper), 70, *92*, *93*